OUTDOORS

SO-CEW-354

BAY AREA BIKING

ANN MARIE BROWN

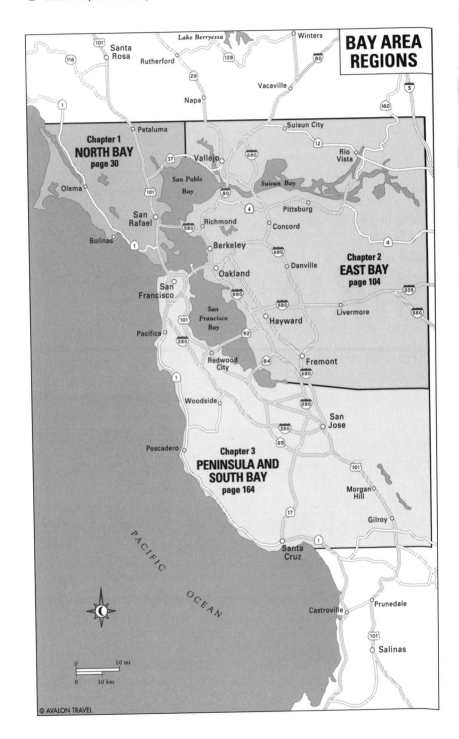

Contents

❰ Best Rides for Families   ❰ Best Waterfront Rides
❰ Best Rides to High Overlooks   ❰ Best Rides for Wildlife-Viewing
❰ Best Single-Track Rides

Chapter 3

How to Use This Book

ABOUT THE MAPS

This book is divided into chapters based on regions; an overview map of these regions precedes the table of contents. Each chapter begins with a region map that shows the locations and numbers of the rides listed in that chapter. Each ride profile is also accompanied by a detailed map that shows the bike route.

Map Symbols

————	Road Route	○	City
--------	Unpaved Road Route	○	Town
------	Trail Route	**℗**	Trailhead Parking
—·—·—	Optional Route	Start	Start of Ride
----------	Trail	▪	Point of Interest
....	Trail (Bikes Prohibited)	★	Natural Feature
══════	Divided Highway	▲	Mountain
══════	Primary Road	▲	State Park
══════	Secondary Road	ᴧ	Campground
- - - - - -	Unpaved Road	⬚	Waterfall

ABOUT THE ELEVATION PROFILES

Each profile includes an elevation scale which approximately graphs the hills and dips on the route in height and distance. Please note that the scales on each profile are dramatically different. Scales may not always begin at an elevation of zero feet and height increments and distance can vary.

ABOUT THE RIDE PROFILES

Each profile includes a narrative description of the ride's setting and terrain. This description also includes mile-by-mile route directions, as well as information about the ride's highlights and unique attributes.

The rides marked by the **BEST ◖** symbol are highlighted in the author's Best Bike Rides list.

Options

If alternative routes are available, this section is used to provide information on side trips or note how to shorten or lengthen the ride.

Driving Directions

This section provides detailed driving directions to the start of the route from the nearest major town.

Route Directions

Each profile includes a mile-by-mile listing of what to expect along the trail or road. Every major turn is noted and nearby sights or supplies are indicated where available.

ABOUT THE DIFFICULTY RATING

Each profile includes a difficulty rating. The level of difficulty for any trail can change considerably due to weather or trail conditions. Always phone ahead to check on current trail and weather conditions. The ratings are defined as follows:

1: Suitable for families with young children, novice riders, or those wanting a casual recreational ride. They include both road rides and mountain bike rides that are nearly level and are usually less than 15 miles or have shorter options. Trail surfaces are smooth and most are on bike paths where there is no vehicular traffic.

2: These rides are suitable for families with older children and for strong beginners, i.e. novices who are physically fit. Road rides are generally less than 25 miles and have little elevation gain. Off-road rides may involve some varied surfaces but don't require technical mountain biking skills. Bikers should expect to ride on dirt or grassy trails, dirt roads, and a variety of surfaces.

3: These rides are appropriate for people with solid aerobic fitness and some cycling experience. Road rides are generally less than 30 miles and involve moderate hill climbs. Mountain bike rides will require some basic technical skills, such as the ability to ride over and around rough surfaces (rocks, roots, ruts, water obstacles), descend hills, maneuver through tight turns, follow a narrow line with good balance, etc. Bikers should have moderate experience on a variety of trails, including single-track.

4: These rides are suitable for intermediate riders with excellent aerobic fitness. Road rides are generally 20-40 miles long and involve some steep hill-climbing. Mountain bike rides require technical skills, involve some steep hill climbs and descents, and call for good bike handling skills. Bikers should have solid experience on a variety of trails, including single-track.

5: These are challenging rides for experienced cyclists with excellent aerobic fitness. Road rides have several steep or prolonged hill climbs, and some routes are more than 50 miles. Mountain bike rides are technical, on a variety of surfaces and types of trails, require advanced bike handling skills, may have cyclocross sections, and generally include steep climbs and descents.

INTRODUCTION

Author's Note

When I see an adult on a bicycle, I do not despair for the future of the human race.
—H. G. Wells

It used to be that bicyclists fell into two categories: road cyclists and mountain bikers. The former spent a lot of money on bikes that weighed less than a full water bottle and black Spandex tights that fit like a second skin. They joined cycling clubs and milled around with their compatriots at coffee shops on Sunday mornings, drinking lattes and studying road maps before the day's ride.

The latter saw themselves as rebels, riding fat-tire bikes that were often splattered with mud. They wore baggy shorts and hiking boots, and were frequently heard yelling "yahoo" (or something similar) as they cleaned a boulder-lined descent or bunny-hopped over a fallen log. They coined their own phrases, like "eat rocks" and "dual-boing suspension."

At different phases of my life, I have been a card-carrying member of one group or the other. I pedaled century rides on a 19-pound skinny-tire wonder—a jerry-rigged, hand-me-down relic that was coveted by other riders for its all-Campy components. I searched out long and winding country roads and rode them in the good company of friends. In my best moments, I felt like I was a member of the peloton riding in the Tour de France.

Then, after moving to San Francisco and later to Marin County, I switched over to mountain bikes and cruised around the hills and dales of Northern California. I learned the difference between serpentine and granite and schist, and what it feels like to ride on, over, and around those marvelous rocks. I spotted red-tailed hawks and golden eagles, and shared the trails with deer, bears, and bobcats. In my best moments, I felt like I was using a two-wheeled machine to get closer to nature, to travel farther than I could on foot and visit places where automobiles could not go.

It never occurred to me that the twain could ever meet—that my two bicycling selves could shake hands and coexist happily. But somewhere inside, a small voice was seeking integration. Why be one thing and not the other? Why not embrace the two biking sports as one? And so this book was born. To me, the beauty of bicycling is its wind-in-the-hair, feeling-like-a-kid-again euphoria, which can be achieved on either road or trail. It is knowing that no matter what ails you in the rest of life—monotonous job, unrequited love, too much housework—all you need do is get on your bike and pedal and everything will feel better.

The 60 rides in this book, plus multiple options and add-ons, celebrate the all-in-one joy of both road biking and mountain biking. Whether you own both types of bikes or only one or the other, you will find a wealth of rides in these pages that suit your desires and ability level.

Inevitably, you'll also discover my personal biases for scenery and serenity. On trail rides, you'll find waterfalls, ocean views, redwood forests, and summit vistas. (I don't enjoy grinding out miles just for the sake of it.) On paved rides, you'll find more of the same, plus wide shoulders and as few cars as possible. (I don't like riding next to cars that fly by at 60 mph, shaving my legs with hot exhaust.) My guiding rule for choosing bike routes is this: With every ride, on road or trail, I like to return home feeling like I've done something extraordinary with my day.

Happy riding to you.

Best Bike Rides

Of the 60 road and trail rides in this book, here are my favorites in five categories:

◖ Best Rides for Families

Bear Valley Trail Bike and Hike, North Bay, page 41. This excursion in Point Reyes National Seashore is easy enough for cyclists of any ability, and it leads to a spectacular coastal overlook.

Perimeter Trail and Fire Road Loops, North Bay, page 94. The 5.5-mile, nearly level Perimeter Trail circumnavigates Angel Island in the middle of San Francisco Bay, providing outstanding views and some interesting history lessons.

Nimitz Way and Wildcat Canyon, East Bay, page 106. Perched on the tip of San Pablo Ridge in Tilden Park, Nimitz Way Trail offers the best views of any paved trail in the east San Francisco Bay.

Sawyer Camp Recreation Trail, Peninsula and South Bay, page 172. This trail in the pristine San Francisco Watershed near Hillsborough travels the length of Lower Crystal Springs Reservoir and leads through marshlands to southern San Andreas Lake.

Berry Creek Falls Bike and Hike, Peninsula and South Bay, page 225. A 11.6-mile round-trip bike ride in Big Basin Redwoods State Park brings you to a short hike to one of the Bay Area's most spectacular waterfalls.

◖ Best Rides to High Overlooks

Stinson Beach and Mount Tamalpais Loop, North Bay, page 76. Starting from sea level at Stinson Beach, ride to the 2,571-foot summit of Mount Tamalpais's East Peak on scenic back roads.

Old Stage Road and Old Railroad Grade to East Peak, North Bay, page 79. Take a ride through Mount Tamalpais history on the old Mount Tamalpais Scenic Railway route, then enjoy panoramic views from the mountain's East Peak.

Mount Diablo Summit Ride, East Bay, page 137. You haven't experienced Mount Diablo's Summit Road until you've ridden it on a bike—all the way to the mountain summit at 3,849 feet, where you can see as far as the Sierra Nevada.

Montara Mountain, Peninsula and South Bay, page 169. Pick a clear day for this mountain-bike ride to the summit of 1,898-foot Montara Mountain, where you'll be rewarded with dazzling views of the Pacific coast.

Mount Hamilton, Peninsula and South Bay, page 216. Climb to the top of the Bay Area's loftiest peak, Mount Hamilton at 4,209 feet, where astronomers at Lick Observatory keep a watch on the stars.

◖ Best Single-Track Rides

Tamarancho Loop, North Bay, page 64. You have to pay for a permit to ride at the Boy Scouts' Camp Tamarancho near Fairfax, but this seven-mile single-track loop is well worth the fee.

China Camp Bay View Loop, North Bay, page 70. A rarity in the state park system, China Camp State Park permits mountain biking on many miles of trails, including some gorgeous single-track stretches through the forest and alongside San Pablo Bay.

El Corte de Madera Creek Loop, Peninsula and South Bay, page 180. A wide variety of trails, including plenty of challenging single-track, tunnel through a dense forest of redwoods and Douglas firs at this Skyline Boulevard open-space preserve.

Saratoga Gap Loop, Peninsula and South Bay, page 207. Peninsula mountain bikers head for this 12.9-mile loop through three contiguous parklands to sharpen their single-track skills.

Middle Ridge Loop, Peninsula and South Bay, page 222. It isn't easy riding in this steep, hilly park, but Henry W. Coe State Park is known to have some of the best single-track in the Bay Area.

◖ Best Waterfront Rides

Cheese Company and Tomales Bay Loop, North Bay, page 35. Stop for a lunch of fresh oysters as you pedal a nine-mile stretch alongside Tomales Bay.

Tiburon and Belvedere Loop, North Bay, page 85. This easy road ride circles around the Tiburon Peninsula and Belvedere, passing multimillion-dollar homes and providing priceless bay views.

Perimeter Trail and Fire Road Loops, North Bay, page 94. There is no place in the Bay Area where you can enjoy more blue-water views than on Angel Island, set smack in the middle of San Francisco Bay.

Golden Gate Bridge and Marin Headlands Loop, North Bay, page 97. Ride across the Golden Gate Bridge, visit the Point Bonita Lighthouse, and stop at Black Sand and Rodeo Beaches on this remarkable coastal loop route.

Pescadero and San Gregorio Loop, Peninsula and South Bay, page 197.

Pedal south on coastal Highway 1 past Pigeon Point Lighthouse and Whaler's Cove, then loop back through the historic towns of Pescadero and San Gregorio.

◖ Best Rides for Wildlife-Viewing

Estero Trail, North Bay, page 38. The pasturelands of Point Reyes are home to much more than cows; bring your binoculars on this trip to take advantage of ample bird-watching opportunities, including owls, egrets, and herons.

Point Reyes Lighthouse, North Bay, page 44. From December to April, spot gray whales from the Point Reyes Lighthouse coastal promontory and observe elephant seals from an overlook at nearby Chimney Rock.

Stinson Beach and Mount Tamalpais Loop, North Bay, page 76. From mid-March to mid-July, see hundreds of pairs of great egrets nesting in the trees at Bolinas Lagoon.

Alameda Creek Trail, East Bay, page 157. You may notice a few birds as you ride alongside Alameda Creek, but when you reach the trail's end at Coyote Hills Regional Park, you're in some of the best bird-watching territory in the Bay Area.

Sawyer Camp Recreation Trail, Peninsula and South Bay, page 172. You'll have an excellent chance of spotting deer, hawks, herons, and egrets in various spots along this paved trail that skirts the edge of Lower Crystal Springs Reservoir.

Biking Tips

BIKING ESSENTIALS

Like the Boy Scout motto says: "Be prepared." It's easy to set off on a bike ride, especially on a trail or road near your home, carrying nothing except your wallet and keys. We've all done it from time to time. But even on the shortest spin through the neighborhood or local park, it's wise to have a few items with you. Some riders carry all of the following items on every ride, some carry only some of the items some of the time. But each of these could prove to be a real lifesaver.

Helmet

They don't call them "brain buckets" for nothing. Don't get on your bike without one; many parks require them, and the ones that don't, should. Just as you wear your seat belt when you drive, wear your helmet when you ride. Make sure yours fits properly and strap it on securely. If you are a woman rider, buy a women's helmet. It will fit your head much better, and a better fit equals better protection for your head.

Food and Water

Being hungry or thirsty spoils a good time, and it can also turn into a potentially dangerous situation. Even if you aren't the least bit hungry or thirsty when you start, you will feel completely different after 30 minutes of riding. Always carry

©ANN MARIE BROWN

Point Reyes Lighthouse

BIKE MAINTENANCE 101

Most of us wouldn't think of neglecting the basic maintenance services our cars need. We fill up our gas tanks, clean our windshields, check our tire pressure, change the oil every few thousand miles, and even treat our cars to a complete tune-up now and then. Our bicycles need to be cared for with the same attentiveness, but too often they aren't. They sit unused in the garage all winter, then on the first sunny spring morning, we impatiently take them out for a spin without so much as checking the tire inflation.

It doesn't take the mind of a mechanic or a workbench full of fancy tools to keep your wheels in tip-top shape. A few clean rags, some lubricant, chain cleaning fluid, and simple tools like a set of Allen wrenches, a tire pump with an accurate gauge, one flathead and one Phillips screwdriver, tire levers (also called tire irons), and pliers will take care of the basics. Riders who want to do more than elementary maintenance will also want a spoke wrench, a chain tool, and a stand to support the bicycle while it is being worked on.

How often should your bike be serviced? It depends on how often and where you ride. Fair-weather riders who stick to paved trails and roads have less maintenance to do than mountain bikers who like to get out in the dirt and mud. Bikes that are ridden three or more times a week need a lot more care than bikes that rarely leave the garage. The following guidelines serve as an "average" maintenance schedule that should be sufficient for most recreational riders:

Before every ride: Check the tire pressure; if it is low, add air. While you're at it, check the tire sidewalls and treads for wear. Make sure that the treads are free of debris. Check that the quick-release levers on your wheel(s)

at least two water bottles on your bike, and make sure they are full of fresh, clean water when you head out. Add ice on hot days, if you wish. For a two- to three-hour ride, 100 ounces of water is not overkill, especially in summer. Many riders prefer to wear a bladder-style backpack hydration system, which has the extra advantage of providing room to carry a few snacks or car keys. Always bring some food with you, even if it's just a couple of energy bars. If you carry extras to share, you'll be the hero or heroine when you give them to a rider in need.

Clothing

Cycling shorts and cycling gloves will make your trip a lot more comfortable. Cycling gloves have padded palms so the nerves in your hands are protected from the pressure of leaning your upper body weight on the handlebars. Cycling shorts have synthetic chamois or other padding in the saddle area, and it's obvious what function that serves. Look for a bike short with six-panel (or greater) construction—more panels generally equals a more comfortable fit.

On the trail, weather and temperature conditions can change at any time. It may get windy or start to rain, or you can get too warm as you ride uphill in the are securely fastened. Squeeze both sets of brakes to see if they are working well, and check that the brake pads are squarely hitting the rims, not the tires. Spin the wheels around a few times to make sure they are properly aligned, not wobbling or out of true. Take a look at your chain and derailleurs; if they appear dry, add a touch of lubricant. Wipe off the excess with a rag. If you have clipless pedals, check that they are clean and free of debris so that you can clip in and out efficiently. And, although it seems obvious, don't forget to rinse out your water bottles and refill them.

Every 500 miles or once a month: Wipe off your bike with a rag and inspect the frame and fork for cracks or signs of wear. Clean the chain with a degreaser and then relubricate it. Check the wheel spokes to make sure that none are loose. Use a wrench to check all bolts and screws for tightness. Don't neglect the bolts on the seatpost, stem, handlebars, crank arms, and pedals. Lubricate the cables, brakes, derailleurs, and rotating points on the pedals. If you have suspension components on your bike, check the owner's manual to see how and when the shocks should be lubricated and maintained.

Every 2,500 miles or six months: Check and replace your tires and brake pads if needed. Check all cables for rust, fraying, or wear, and replace as needed. Clean the entire drive train (chain, chainrings, cassette, front and rear derailleurs) with an appropriate solvent. Replace the chain if needed.

Every 5,000 miles or once a year: Take your bike into a bike shop and let an experienced mechanic give it the once-over. For a nominal cost, you'll be able to rest assured that your bike is in great condition for another year of safe and happy riding.

sun and then too cold as you ride downhill in the shade. Wear layers. Bring a lightweight jacket and a rain poncho with you. Tie your extra clothes around your waist or put them in a small daypack.

Maps

Sometimes trails and roads are signed, sometimes they're not. Signs get knocked down or disappear with alarming frequency, due to rain, wind, or souvenir hunters. Get a map from the managing agency of the park you're visiting; all their names and phone numbers are listed in this book. For road rides, take along a detailed AAA or other map for the region. A GPS device can be quite handy, too, especially on road rides.

Repair Kit

How many and which tools to carry is a great subject of debate. At the very least, if you're going to be farther than easy walking distance from your car, carry what you need to fix a flat tire. Great distances are covered quickly on a bike. This is never more apparent than when a tire goes flat 30 minutes into a ride and it

ACHIEVING PROPER BIKE FIT

It doesn't matter if you ride a $300 bike or a $3,000 bike – if your machine doesn't fit your body, you will be unhappy with your ride. Proper bike fit takes into account the three major areas where your bike and body connect: at your feet, hands, and seat. A bike that doesn't fit right is harder to control, and riding an ill-fitting bike for an extended period of time can lead to aches and pains in the lower back, hips, knees, neck, and shoulders.

The first element of proper bike fit is known as "stand-over height." It is easily checked by simply straddling the bike with both feet on the ground while wearing your usual biking shoes, and then bouncing up and down on your heels. If your crotch touches the frame, the bike is too big for you; you need a bike with a smaller frame size. Minimum stand-over height for riding on pavement is 2 inches. For mountain biking, minimum stand-over height is 3-4 inches.

If your bike's stand-over height is sufficient, the next thing you should check is your saddle position. Saddles can be adjusted in three directions: up and down, forward and back, and angle of tilt. The most important adjustment is height (up or down). Many people ride with their saddles too high, because they believe it gives their legs more power. Over time, this can lead to injuries of the hips, knees, or back. To test for correct seat height, take your shoes off. Have a friend hold your bike steady while you sit on the saddle and turn the pedals until one is all the way up and the other is all the way down. Your bare heel (not your toes) should rest easily on the downward pedal without having to adjust or rock your hips. Your knee should be just slightly bent. Your friend can tell you if you are rocking your hips in order to reach the pedal with your heel. If so, lower your saddle.

Forward and back adjustment, and angle of tilt, are more subjective matters. It is best to start with your seat adjusted so it is in the middle of its rails and horizontal, then make minor adjustments to see what is most comfortable for you. Some bike shops insist that the best way to make a fore/aft adjustment on the saddle is to drop a plumb

©ANN MARIE BROWN

line from the hinge of your knee to your pedal axle, but there is a simpler test: After riding for a few hours, if you find that your arms and shoulders are tired, you may be balancing too much of your weight on your handlebars and front wheel. Try moving your seat back on its rails, which will put more of your weight in your saddle.

Because many bicycle seats are narrow, hard, and just plain uncomfortable, many riders insist on tilting the nose of the saddle down to "take the pressure off." If you feel you have to have a downward saddle tilt to make your ride comfortable, consider buying another saddle. No amount of padding in your cycling shorts can make up for a poorly made or poorly fitting saddle. Women in particular should try out the wider saddles on the market, which are designed for the wider female pelvis. Many even come with a cutout section in the middle, or a foam insert, to take pressure off the pubic bone.

The next important component of bike fit is the height and angle of your handlebars, which is closely related to the adjustment of your saddle. As a general rule, your handlebars should be set at approximately the same height as your saddle. But if your torso and arms are particularly long or short, you may want to raise or lower the handlebars to accommodate your reach. Here's a simple test to check the fit of your handlebars: Standing next to your bike, touch the back of your elbow to the front of your saddle. Place your forearm parallel to the ground, with your fingers reaching toward the handlebars. Your fingertips should come within 2–4 inches of the handlebars. If the distance is greater, you are reaching too far while riding. Get a shorter handlebar stem, tilt your handlebars, move your saddle slightly forward, or try any combination of these three adjustments. Pay attention to your hands on longer rides; if you find yourself sitting up and steering with the tips of your fingers, your "reach" needs adjustment. On the other hand, if your handlebars are too low, you will have to strain to keep your head up and your eyes on the road, and your neck and upper back will be tense or uncomfortable when you ride.

Finally, the positioning of your brake and shifting levers should be in sync with the size of your hands and fingers. If you have small hands and find it difficult to reach the brake or shift levers, change the position of the controls on the handlebars.

Women riders who are considering a new bike purchase should give some serious thought to buying a women-specific frame. Almost every major bike manufacturer now makes women-specific bikes. While some simply modify a stock "unisex" frame by switching to a shorter stem, smaller handlebars, shorter cranks, and a wider saddle, others take a more comprehensive approach, taking into account that the average woman (and there are plenty of exceptions to "average") has a shorter torso, shorter arms, and longer legs than a man of the same height. Also, a woman's hands and feet are usually smaller, her shoulders are narrower, and her hips are wider than a comparably sized man. For many female riders, having a frame that was designed with women-specific geometry makes a huge difference in terms of bike handling and power. But remember that not all women are built the same; for some, a man's frame may fit just fine. Always test-ride a variety of different types of bikes before handing over your hard-earned cash.

takes two hours to walk back. So why walk? Carry a spare tube, a patch kit, tire levers, and a bike pump attached to your bike frame. Make sure you know how to use them.

Many riders also carry a small set of metric wrenches, Allen wrenches, and a couple of screwdrivers, or some type of all-in-one bike tool. These are good for adjusting derailleurs and the angle on your bike seat, making minor repairs, and fidgeting with brake and gear cables. If you're riding on dirt trails, carry extra chain lubricant with you, or at least keep some in your car. Some riders carry a few additional tools, such as a spoke wrench for tightening loose spokes or a chain tool to fix a broken chain.

Sunscreen and Sunglasses

Wear both. Apply sunscreen 30 minutes before you go outdoors so it has time to take effect and reapply often—at least every two hours, more frequently if you are perspiring.

Bike Lock

It comes in handy if you want to stop for anything. Many of the trails in this book combine a bike ride with a short hike or a visit to a winery, museum, or historic site. If you are planning to stop anywhere, even to use a restroom, a bike lock is valuable. Never leave your bike unlocked and unattended.

First Aid and Emergencies

Like most of life, bicycling is a generally safe activity that in the mere bat of an eye can become hazardous. The unexpected occurs—a rock in the trail, a sudden change in road surface, a misjudgment or momentary lack of attention—and suddenly, you and your bike are sprawled on the ground. Sooner or later it happens to everyone who rides. Usually, you look around nervously to see if anybody saw you, dust yourself off, and get back on your bike. But it's wise to carry a few emergency items just in case your accident is more serious: A few large and small Band-Aids, antibiotic cream, and an Ace bandage can be valuable tools. I also carry a Swiss Army knife, one with several blades, a can opener, and scissors. If I don't need it for first aid, I'll use it for bike repairs or picnics. Finally, it's a good idea to carry matches in a waterproof container and a candle, just in case you ever need to build a fire in a serious emergency.

Some riders carry a cell phone everywhere they go, but be forewarned that this is not a foolproof emergency device. You won't get cell reception in some areas, particularly in nonurban places. Carry a cell phone and hope it will work, but don't rely on it.

Always bring along a few bucks so you can make a phone call from a pay phone or buy food or drinks for yourself or someone who needs them.

MOUNTAIN BIKING BASICS

First-time mountain bike riders are always surprised at how much time they spend walking instead of riding. They walk their bike up steep grades, down steep grades, and in level places where the terrain is too rugged. Mountain bikers frequently have to deal with rocks, boulders, tree roots, sand traps, holes in the ground, stream crossings, eroded trails, and so on. Often the best way to deal with these obstacles is to walk and push your bike. Becoming familiar with these and other basics of the trail can help ensure a fun ride, instead of a frustrating one.

- If something looks scary, dismount and walk. If you are unsure of your ability to stay in control while heading downhill or your capacity to keep your balance on a rough surface, dismount and walk. It will save you plenty of Band-Aids.
- Learn to shift gears before you need to. This takes some practice, but you'll soon find that it's easier to shift before you're halfway up the hill and the pedals and chain are under pressure. When you see a hill coming up ahead, downshift.
- Play around with the height of your seat. When the seat is properly adjusted, you will have a slight bend in your knee while your leg is fully extended on the lower of the two pedals.
- Take it easy on the handlebar grips. Many beginners squeeze the daylights out of their handlebars, which leads to hand, arm, shoulder, and upper back discomfort. Grip the handlebars loosely and keep a little bend in your elbows.
- Learn to read the trail ahead of you, especially on downhills. Keep your eyes open for rocks or ruts, which can take you by surprise and upset your balance.
- Go slowly. As long as you never exceed the speed at which you feel comfortable and in control, you'll be fine. This doesn't mean that you shouldn't take a few chances, but it's unwise to take chances until you are ready.
- Experienced riders can maneuver their bikes on nearly any terrain, but good technical ability also means managing your speed. Especially when riding on trails shared by hikers, dogs, and horses, it's important to use brakes wisely. Brake before you enter turns or corners so you can ride through them *without* braking. Braking during a turn or curve causes you to lock up your rear wheel and skid or slide. Sliding lessens your control over the bike and is very destructive to the trail. Ride it; don't slide it, or you'll make yourself very unpopular with people who love trails.
- Use the front brake simultaneously and in combination with the back brake to slow you down. But don't pull too hard on the front brake or you'll go over the handlebars. Remember that 70 percent of your braking force is in your front brake.
- Learn to move your weight back and lift up your front wheel to get it over obstacles,

FIXING A FLAT

There's no reason for a flat tire to ruin your ride. If you carry the proper tools with you when you ride, a flat tire will cause you only a few minutes' delay – just enough time to get out of the saddle, take a good look at the scenery, and enjoy a short breather.

Two things to keep in mind: First, remember that most flat tires are directly or indirectly caused by improper inflation (not enough air pressure). If you check your tire pressure before every ride and add air if necessary, you will have fewer flat tires. Second, make sure you are prepared to deal with a flat if you get one. Always carry a new tube, a patch kit, a set of plastic tire levers (also called tire irons), and a pump. The total weight of these items is far less than one pound.

If a tire goes flat, *stop riding immediately*, before you damage your wheel rims. Then, remove the remaining air in the "bad" tire by pressing on the valve and squeezing the tire. Take the wheel off the bike. If you have quick-release levers on your wheels, you're in luck. If not, you'll need to carry a wrench with you to release the wheel nuts. You'll also probably have to disconnect the brake cables on the affected wheel. To do so, squeeze the brakes together, then unhook the brake cable.

Now, consider the most elementary of tire-fixing facts: You don't really have a flat tire, you have a flat tube, which is the rubber circular "thing" that is inside your bike's tire. So you have to get access to that tube. Insert one tire lever between the metal rim and the exterior tire, being careful not to pinch the inner tube. Insert the other tire lever about two inches away from the first (on the same side of the wheel) and push down on both. The tire will start to pop off the rim. Work your way around the tire until one edge of it is completely off the rim. Push the valve stem through the rim and the tube will come out of the tire.

At this juncture you have two choices. If you're in a rush, you can simply replace the punctured tube with the spare tube you brought with you. Before doing so, *carefully* feel around the inside of the tire to make sure that the flat-causing glass, metal, wire, or thorn isn't still in there, or you'll get another flat as soon as you start riding. If you can't find any foreign debris, check the wheel itself for sharp spots and to make sure none of the spokes are poking through. Partially inflate the tube so that you can reinsert it into the tire. Start by inserting the valve stem into the valve hole, then use your fingers to tuck the tube into

like rocks or bumps. Otherwise, your front wheel can get trapped, causing you to fly over the handlebars. Your back wheel will usually roll over obstacles.

- Lean inside and forward into turns and curves. This keeps your center of gravity over your tires.
- On downhills, get your rear end as far back on the bike as possible—behind the seat and over the back tire if you can on extreme downhill pitches.
- When you are approaching a long, steep downhill, stop for a moment and lower your seat. You want to be able to stand on your pedals in a crouched position without the seat getting in the way.

the tire. Don't let it twist or fold back on itself.

Work one side of the tire back onto the wheel rim, preferably using only your fingers (use your tire lever only if desperate). Then do the other side, being careful not to pinch the tube. If you are having trouble getting the tire back on the rim, let some air out of the tube. When it's back together, put the wheel back on the bike, fully inflate the tire, put the valve cap back on, and reconnect the brake cable. Voilà! You are ready to ride.

Or, if you'd rather fix the punctured tube, examine it carefully to find the hole. If you can't see it, pump up the tube and hold it close to your cheek or lips until you can "feel" the spot from which the air is escaping. Some riders swear by over-inflating the tube, which makes it easier to find the puncture. When you find it, mark the spot with a pen or tape so you don't lose it again. Now, follow the directions in your patch kit exactly. Patience and attention to detail are key to getting a good patch. Most kits come with a small file or piece of sandpaper to "rough up" the area surrounding the puncture. Don't skip this step, as it helps the patch glue to adhere. Also, make sure you wait the required time for the glue to set up before applying the patch, or it won't stick well. Apply plenty of pressure, and hold the pressure for the prescribed length of time. A properly applied patch will last forever and is often the strongest part of the tube. A tube with multiple patches can actually be stronger than a brand-new tube! Last but not least, make sure you remove the flat-causing culprit from the inside of the tire before reinserting your newly patched tube, as described above.

If you get a lot of flat tires, ask yourself if you are checking your tire inflation before you ride. If you still get lots of flats, consider installing a tire liner made of Kevlar between the tube and the tire. Or you can purchase thorn-resistant tubes, which are thicker than regular tubes. Both options will weigh down your wheels somewhat, but if you're cycling in the cactus-ridden desert, it might be worth it. A product called Slime is another good flat-fighter; it's a nontoxic solution you put inside your tires that automatically seals small punctures. Finally, Specialized makes a brand of tires called Armadillo, which are basically bullet-proof, although they do result in a somewhat harsher ride. Armadillo tires are available for both road and mountain bikes in a huge variety of styles designed for various conditions (hardpack, loam, pavement, multi-terrain, etc.).

• Never ride in mud; your tire tracks will encourage erosion. Walk your bike around muddy areas; don't ride around them and create an even wider trail.

ON THE TRAIL
Mountain Biking Etiquette

Mountain bikes are great. They give you an alternative to pavement, a way out of the concrete jungle. They guarantee your freedom from auto traffic. They take you into the woods and the wild, to places of natural beauty.

On the other hand, mountain bikes are the cause of a lot of controversy. In the

view from Perimeter Trail, Angel Island State Park

past 20 years, mountain bikers have shown up on trails that were once the exclusive domain of hikers and horseback riders. Some say the peace and quiet has been shattered. Some say that trail surfaces are being ruined by the weight and force of mountain bikes. Some say that mountain bikes are too fast and clumsy to share the trail with other types of users.

Much of the debate can be resolved if bikers follow a few simple rules, and if nonbikers practice a little tolerance. The following are guidelines for low-impact, "soft cycling." If you obey them, you'll help to give mountain biking the good name it deserves:

1. Ride only on trails where bikes are permitted. Obey all signs and trail closures.
2. Yield to equestrians. Horses can be badly spooked by bicyclists, so give them plenty of room. If horses are approaching you, stop alongside the trail until they pass. If horses are traveling in your direction and you need to pass them, call out politely to the rider and ask permission. If the horse moves off the trail and the rider tells you it's okay, then pass.
3. Yield to hikers. Bikers travel much faster than hikers. Understand that you have the potential to scare the daylights out of hikers as you speed downhill around a curve and overtake them from behind, or when you race at them head-on. Make sure you give other trail users plenty of room, and keep your speed down when you are near them. If you see a hiker, slow down to a crawl, or even stop.

4. Be as friendly and polite as possible. Potential ill will can be eliminated by friendly greetings as you pass: "Hello, beautiful day today... " Always say thank you to other trail users for allowing you to pass.
5. Avoid riding on wet trails. Bike tires leave ruts in wet soil that accelerate erosion. This makes bikers very unpopular with park managers and other trail users. Don't ride a trail immediately after a downpour or, in places like Tahoe and Shasta, too soon after snowmelt.
6. Riders going downhill should always yield to riders going uphill on narrow trails. Get out of their way so they can keep their momentum as they climb.

Protecting the Outdoors

Take good care of this beautiful land you're riding on. The primary rules are to leave no trace of your visit, to pack out all your trash, and to try not to disturb animal or plant life. But you can go the extra mile and pick up any litter that you see on the trail or road. Carry an extra bag to hold the litter you collect until you get to a trash receptacle, or just keep an empty pocket for that purpose.

If you have the extra time or energy, you can join a trail organization in your area or spend some time volunteering in your local park. Biking and hiking trails need constant upkeep and maintenance, and most of the work gets done by volunteers. Anything you do to help this lovely planet will be repaid to you, many times over.

NORTH BAY

© ANN MARIE BROWN

BEST BIKE RIDES

Whether your tastes run to fat tires or skinny

tires, Campagnolo or Rockshox, Marin County and the surrounding North Bay is an undisputed mecca for cyclists. Home to thousands of pairs of well-toned legs, closets full of black Lycra shorts, and countless miles of dirt and paved trails, the North Bay affords a world of opportunities for mountain bikers, road cyclists, and recreational riders of all types.

The North Bay has all the right ingredients for cycling nirvana: winding country roads with only the most mellow car traffic, mild weather with plenty of sun but not too much heat, a jaw-dropping stretch of rugged Pacific coast, world-famous landmarks like the Golden Gate Bridge and Point Reyes Lighthouse, and even Mount Tamalpais, the self-proclaimed birthplace of mountain biking. It was on Mount Tam's steep slopes that Gary Fisher, Joe Breeze, and their compatriots held the first formal off-road bike races in the late 1970s. Those first mountain bikes were heavy, clunky, and downright dangerous, but a few years and a few modifications later, mountain bike fever caught on and an industry was born.

Several park agencies in the North Bay are particularly friendly to mountain bikers. The Golden Gate National Recreation Area and Point Reyes National Seashore allow bikes on many of their trails – a rarity in the national park system. Several state parks do the same, including Mount

Tamalpais, Angel Island, and China Camp, the latter being a particular favorite of fat-tire riders because they are permitted on its single-track trails as well as its wide fire roads. From many points in the North Bay, the tall buildings of San Francisco can be spotted in the distance, and yet with all this uninhabited parkland where bikers are free to roam, the city seems a world away.

Perhaps the best part about riding the roads and trails of the North Bay is that there is so much to do besides pedal. Munch on fresh oysters in Marshall and locally produced cheeses in Nicasio. Watch for whale spouts or stop for lunch along the shores of Drakes Bay. Visit a coastal waterfall, a black-sand beach, or a dwarf grove of cypress trees. While away a few rest stops in quaint country hamlets like Tomales, Point Reyes Station, Valley Ford, and Inverness. Step back in time at a 19th-century Chinese shrimp-fishing village at China Camp, tour two historic lighthouses perched along the precipitous Marin coast, or visit an immigrant detention center on an island in the middle of San Francisco Bay. A surprising range of side trips and activities are available, but then again, plenty of riders are happy just to spin their wheels and take in the extraordinary North Bay scenery. It's the region's scenic beauty more than any other feature that compels people to get on their bikes and ride.

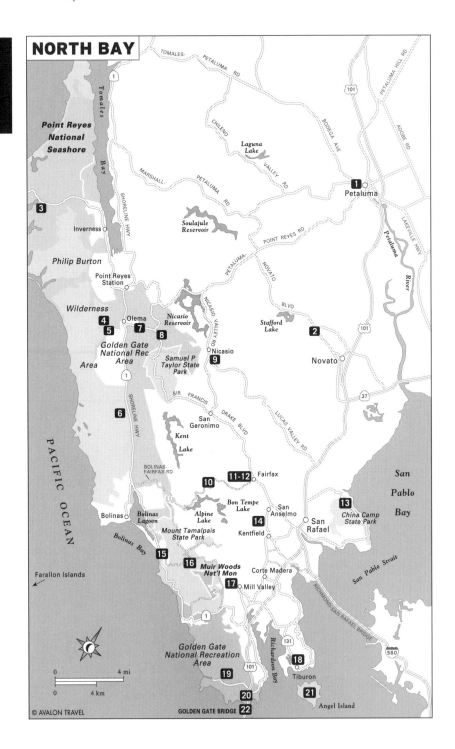

TRAIL NAME	LEVEL	DISTANCE	TIME	ELEVATION	PAGE
1 Petaluma and Dillon Beach Ramble	3	55.3 mi	4 hr	1,800 ft	32
2 Cheese Company and Tomales Bay Loop	3	46 mi	3-4 hr	1,800 ft	35
3 Estero Trail	2	12 mi	3 hr	1,200 ft	38
4 Bear Valley Trail Bike and Hike	1	6.2 mi (plus 1.8-mile hike)	2 hr	500 ft	41
5 Point Reyes Lighthouse	3-4	45 mi	3.5-4.5 hr	1,900 ft	44
6 Stewart Trail	4	13 mi	2-3 hr	2,500 ft	48
7 Bolinas Ridge and Olema Valley Loop	2	15 mi	2 hr	1,000 ft	51
8 Cross Marin Trail and Bolinas Ridge Loop	3	13.4 mi	2.5 hr	1,250 ft	54
9 Nicasio Reservoir Loop	2	24.5 mi	2 hr	900 ft	58
10 Pine Mountain Loop	3	13.2 mi	2.5 hr	2,000 ft	61
11 Tamarancho Loop	3	11.7 mi	2 hr	1,000 ft	64
12 Fairfax and Mount Tamalpais Loop	3	31.8 mi	3-4 hr	2,200 ft	67
13 China Camp Bay View Loop	3	11.6 mi	2 hr	600 ft	70
14 Three Lakes Loop	2	11.2 mi	1.5 hr	900 ft	73
15 Stinson Beach and Mount Tamalpais Loop	4	23.9 mi	3 hr	2,700 ft	76
16 Old Stage Road and Old Railroad Grade to East Peak	2	8 mi	1.5 hr	1,100 ft	79
17 Old Railroad Grade to West Point Inn	3	13.8 mi	2 hr	1,700 ft	82
18 Tiburon and Belvedere Loop	2	10.5 mi	1 hr	700 ft	85
19 Tennessee Valley and Coyote Ridge Loop	3	6.5 mi	1.5 hr	1,200 ft	88
20 Marin Headlands Miwok and Bobcat Loop	4	14 mi	2 hr	2,100 ft	91
21 Perimeter Trail and Fire Road Loops	2	9.6 mi	2 hr	900 ft	94
22 Golden Gate Bridge and Marin Headlands Loop	3	15 mi	1.5-2 hr	1,500 ft	97

▮1 PETALUMA AND DILLON BEACH RAMBLE

Petaluma to Dillon Beach, northwest Marin County

PAVED ROADS WITH MINIMAL CAR TRAFFIC

Difficulty: 3   **Total Distance:** 55.3 miles (or 25-mile option)

Riding Time: 4 hours   **Elevation Gain:** 1,800 feet

Summary: Sheep, cows, and llamas are your companions on this Petaluma countryside ride.

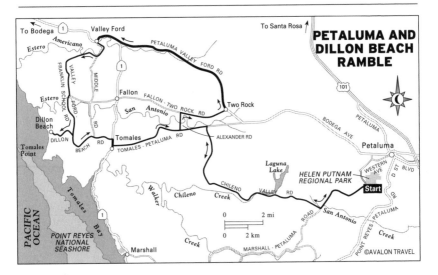

Chileno Valley Road is the long, rambling way to get to the coast from Petaluma, but for bicyclists, it's the obvious choice. The road is filled with small ups and downs, multiple curves and twists, and a whole lot of cows standing beside it and sometimes in it. Few motorists bother with this road; they use the more direct Bodega Avenue instead.

After a 12.6-mile stint on Chileno Valley's bucolic, pasture-lined thorough-fare, this rambling 55-mile ride makes a loop through the small towns of Valley Ford, Dillon Beach, and Tomales. This results in a perfect half-day ride with no killer climbs, but with plenty of great scenery, both in the inland hills and on the windswept coast.

Each of these three towns has an interesting history. Valley Ford was a potato-farming community in the 19th century, but in the 1920s the residents took up sheep farming. Little has changed since then; you'll still see plenty of woolly sheep, plus an abundance of cows and a smattering of llamas. Dillon Beach has been a seaside resort since 1888, when George Dillon constructed a hotel at the end of

Pasture-lined Chileno Valley Road is the rambler's way from Petaluma to the coast.

the West Marin railroad line, hoping to attract city folk to the local beaches and clamming beds. Tomales was a railroad stop in the late 1880s. Today its short main street boasts the revered Tomales Bakery (707/878-2429, www.tomalesbakery.com), which is always worth a calorie-replenishing stop, a general store, and a café and restaurant.

Options

If the mileage on this ride seems intimidating, it is easy enough to cut it into two rides for two separate days: a 25-mile out-and-back on Chileno Valley Road starting from Helen Putnam Regional Park, and a 27-mile loop through Tomales, Dillon Beach, and Valley Ford, starting from any of those towns.

Driving Directions

From U.S. 101 in Petaluma, take the Petaluma Boulevard South exit and drive north 2 miles. Turn left (west) on Western Avenue and drive 2.2 miles, then turn left on Chileno Valley Road and drive 0.8 mile to Helen Putnam Regional Park on the left.

Route Directions

0.0 Park at Helen Putnam Regional Park and ride west on Chileno Valley Road. (Parking is available inside the park or in pullouts along the road.) *Supplies are available in Petaluma.*

3.0 RIGHT to stay on Chileno Valley Road.

12.6 LEFT on Tomales–Petaluma Road.

13.8 RIGHT on Alexander Road.

14.8 RIGHT on Fallon–Two Rock Road.

17.2 LEFT on Petaluma–Valley Ford Road (hamlet of Two Rock).

26.0 LEFT on Valley Ford Estero Road (town of Valley Ford). *Supplies are available.*

31.8 RIGHT on Dillon Beach Road. Ride out and back through Dillon Beach, then TURN AROUND and return to junction with Valley Ford Road. *Supplies are available in Dillon Beach.*

34.6 RIGHT on Dillon Beach Road.

37.2 RIGHT on Shoreline Highway (Highway 1) in town of Tomales. *Supplies are available.*

37.5 LEFT on Tomales–Petaluma Road.

42.7 RIGHT on Chileno Valley Road.

52.3 LEFT to stay on Chileno Valley Road.

55.3 Arrive at starting point.

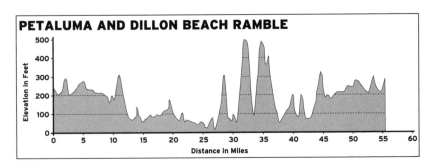

PETALUMA AND DILLON BEACH RAMBLE

2 CHEESE COMPANY AND TOMALES BAY LOOP

BEST **◖**

Novato to Marshall, northwest Marin County

PAVED ROADS WITH MINIMAL CAR TRAFFIC

Difficulty: 3

Total Distance: 46 miles

Riding Time: 3-4 hours

Elevation Gain: 1,800 feet

Summary: This cycling and snacking tour of western Marin County is perfect for road riders.

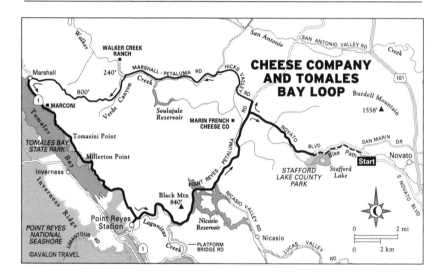

This is a ride for the gourmet cyclist. You'll work up an appetite on this 46-mile ride, then satisfy it with barbecued oysters from Tomales Bay and brie and camembert from the Marin French Cheese Company.

Although Marin County has many scenic road rides, this is one of the loveliest. It offers a mix of pastoral hills and green, fertile valleys, plus level riding along the edge of Tomales Bay. The bucolic charms of this excursion will make you forget you are in the same county (perhaps even in the same country) as the busy corridor of U.S. 101 north of the Golden Gate.

Plus, the loop visits two of west Marin's most charming towns: Marshall and Point Reyes Station. Marshall is known for two things: tranquil bay views and shellfish. More than half of California's oyster and shellfish growers lease acreage on the floor of Tomales Bay. To sample the local mollusks, head for the Hog Island Oyster Company (415/663-9218, www.hogislandoysters.com), Tomales Bay

the start of Marshall–Petaluma Road's demanding two-mile climb

Oyster Company (415/663-1242, tomalesbayoysters.com), or the Marshall Store (415/663-1339, www.themarshallstore.com), all which are located right alongside Highway 1. Don't like oysters? Order the clam chowder.

The quaint town of Point Reyes Station is 0.3 mile off the loop and worth a side trip. The old railroad town features an eclectic mix of shops and cafés, including the ever-popular Bovine Bakery (415/663-9420), purveyor of organic, handmade pastries, which has a crowd of road bikers thronging at its doors every weekend morning.

The ride has two major hills that are worthy of a warning. The first is a two-mile brutal stint on Marshall–Petaluma Road. Although the seldom-traveled road is a beauty, with lots of ups, downs, and winding curves, its one major hill is infamous for bringing cyclists to their knees. Know in advance that the hardest climbing takes place from mile 15.9 to 17.5, in an area called Three Peaks.

With that ascent accomplished, your reward is a euphoric descent to the coast at Marshall, where after snacking on a dozen or more oysters, you'll enjoy nine miles of gentle pedaling along the edge of Tomales Bay. To best enjoy the exquisite water's-edge scenery, plan this ride for a weekday, when you'll contend with a lot fewer cars on Highway 1. Weekends can be very busy here.

After your bayside stint, you can opt for a brief side trip into Point Reyes Station, or just head inland for the final leg to the Marin French Cheese Company (7500 Red Hill Rd., 707/762-6001, www.marinfrenchcheese.com). Tours of the cheese factory are available at 10 A.M., 11 A.M., 12 P.M., and 3 P.M. daily; cheese and other picnic supplies are for sale. On this stretch, you'll face the second big hill, about a mile past Nicasio Reservoir. The ascent is sustained over 1.5 miles, but it's not as bad as the Marshall–Petaluma hill because you know a big round of brie is waiting on the other side. Be sure to take the Cheese Company's factory tour so you can learn how the yummy stuff is made. *Bon appétit.*

Driving Directions

From San Rafael, drive north for 10 miles on U.S. 101 and take the San Marin Drive exit. Drive northwest for 2.7 miles to the intersection of San Marin Drive and Novato Boulevard, where the bike path begins.

Route Directions

0.0 Park at the intersection of San Marin Drive and Novato Boulevard in Novato, then ride west on the bike path that parallels Novato Boulevard. *Supplies are available in Novato.*

2.5 Pass Stafford Lake County Park on the left; bike trail ends and you ride on Novato Boulevard. *Water is available.*

6.2 RIGHT on Petaluma–Point Reyes Road.

6.7 LEFT on Hicks Valley Road.

9.4 LEFT on Marshall–Petaluma Road.

15.9 Start of steepest climb.

17.5 Summit.

20.3 LEFT on Highway 1 in Marshall. *Supplies are available at various restaurants in town, including the Hog Island Oyster Company, Tomales Bay Oyster Company, and the Marshall Store.*

24.3 Tomales Bay Oyster Company on right.

25.1 Tomales Bay State Park/Millerton Point beach and picnic area.

29.2 LEFT on Petaluma–Point Reyes Road. *Or go right to head into town of Point Reyes Station in 0.3 mile.*

33.1 LEFT at junction with Platform Bridge Road.

33.9 Pass Nicasio Reservoir.

39.3 LEFT into Marin French Cheese Company parking lot. *Supplies are available.*

39.7 RIGHT on Novato Boulevard.

43.5 Pick up bike trail at Stafford Lake County Park.

46.0 Arrive at starting point.

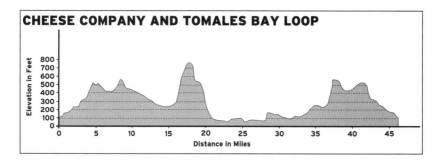

CHEESE COMPANY AND TOMALES BAY LOOP

3 ESTERO TRAIL

BEST ◖

Point Reyes National Seashore

DIRT ROAD AND SINGLE-TRACK

Difficulty: 2

Total Distance: 12 miles

Riding Time: 3 hours

Elevation Gain: 1,200 feet

Summary: Enjoy water-view riding alongside Home Bay and Drakes Estero in the cow pasturelands of Point Reyes.

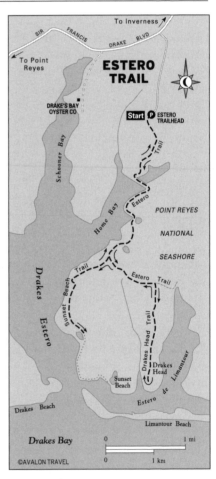

The Estero Trail is quintessential Point Reyes. It's full of good surprises, including an exemplary display of Douglas iris in spring; a dense Monterey pine forest; ample bird-watching opportunities; nonstop views of estuary, bay, and ocean; and access to a pristine beach and high bluff-top overlook. To fully enjoy this excursion, pack a lunch and binoculars and plan on an unhurried ride. The only downside? The route is in cow territory, and the chubby bovines' hooves can make a rutted mess of the old ranch roads, especially in the wet season. It's best to save this ride for summer and fall, after the trails have dried and hardened.

From the parking lot, Estero Trail laterals across a grassy hillside, then rounds a corner and descends into a dense stand of Monterey pines, the tall and aged remains of an old Christmas tree farm and the nesting site of owls and egrets. Shortly the trail opens out to blue, serene Home Bay. A bridge crossing leads you to the first of several short climbs, this one rewarding you with high views of Home Bay's junction with Drakes Estero.

The ride continues parallel to, and mostly high above, the estuary, offering nonstop water views. If the tide is out, mudflats and the oyster beds of nearby

Estero Trail crosses a bridge over Home Bay, then parallels the edge of Drakes Estero.

Drakes Bay Oyster Farm will be revealed. If the tide is in, you'll see miles of azure water. You'll climb and descend a total of three hills on this trail; the third one has a lone eucalyptus tree growing on its summit.

At 2.5 miles, a sign marks Drakes Head to the left and Sunset Beach straight ahead. Turn left and climb through grasslands and chaparral to a confusing maze of cattle gates and fences (watch for arrow signs along the fence). Drakes Head Trail continues southward; the path crosses a coastal prairie and ends on a high bluff overlooking the ocean and Limantour Spit, a long, narrow stretch of sand and grass-covered dunes.

After a pause to enjoy the view, return to the previous junction, then go left on Sunset Beach Trail. The path levels and in 1.5 miles you are within reach of Sunset Beach, where Drakes Estero meets up with Estero de Limantour. A large, quiet pond separates you from the coast, and as the trail continues along the edge of Drakes Estero it soon becomes mucky and impassable for bike tires. Stash your bike and explore beautiful Sunset Beach on foot (best at low tide; consult a tide table for optimal timing).

For more information, contact Point Reyes National Seashore, 415/464-5100, www.nps.gov/pore.

Driving Directions

From San Francisco, cross the Golden Gate Bridge and drive north on U.S. 101 for 7.5 miles. Take the Sir Francis Drake Boulevard exit west toward San Anselmo and drive 20 miles to the town of Olema. At Olema, turn right (north) on Highway 1 for about 150 yards, then turn left on Bear Valley Road. Drive 2.2 miles on Bear Valley Road until it joins with Sir Francis Drake Highway. Bear left on Sir Francis Drake and drive 7.6 miles to the left turnoff for the Estero Trailhead. Turn left and drive 1 mile to the trailhead parking on the right.

Route Directions

0.0 Park at Estero Trailhead. *Supplies are available in the town of Inverness on Sir Francis Drake Highway.*

1.1 Bridge across Home Bay.

2.5 LEFT at junction with Drakes Head Trail (Sunset Beach Trail continues straight).

2.8 Maze of cattle gates, fences, and hiker gates; follow the fence-line path signed with arrows.

3.2 RIGHT on Drakes Head Trail; trail becomes indistinct in places—keep heading south toward the bluff's edge.

4.5 Drakes Head overlook. TURN AROUND.

6.5 LEFT on Sunset Beach Trail at previous junction.

8.0 Arrive at edge of pond with Sunset Beach beyond; stash your bike and explore on foot. TURN AROUND.

12.0 Arrive at starting point.

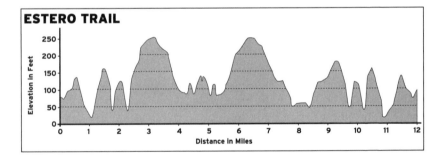

4 BEAR VALLEY TRAIL
BIKE AND HIKE
Point Reyes National Seashore

BEST 🌙

DIRT ROAD

Difficulty: 1

Total Distance: 6.2 miles (plus 1.8-mile hike)

Riding Time: 2 hours

Elevation Gain: 500 feet

Summary: This easy, scenic trip on two wheels and two feet is suitable for the whole family.

Don't forget your bike lock for this short, scenic ride in Point Reyes National Seashore. You'll pedal for 3.1 miles, then hike almost a mile to the top of Arch Rock, a spectacular coastal overlook. Because of this trail's well-deserved popularity, you should time your trip for a weekday or an early morning on the weekend. It's more fun to ride if you aren't dodging a crowd of bikers and hikers.

Beginning just past the Bear Valley Visitor Center and Morgan Horse Ranch, the wide dirt trail is simple to follow. Several side trails intersect Bear Valley Trail but none are open to bikes. Just stay on the main path and cruise beneath the shady forest canopy, comprised of a mix of alders, bay laurel, and fir. At the midway point, after the only noticeable climb of the ride, you'll reach grassy Divide Meadow, a popular picnic spot. Deer are commonly seen here.

At 3.1 miles, the trail reaches a bike rack and several trail junctions. Lock up your bike and continue on foot to Arch Rock. The trail continues

the final steps to Arch Rock on the Bear Valley Trail Bike and Hike

© ANN MARIE BROWN

through the woods for 0.5 mile, following Coast Creek, then suddenly opens out to coastal marshlands. The final steps of the hike are extremely dramatic as you walk along the top of Arch Rock's jagged, jade-green bluff, which juts out over the sea. The wind can howl with tremendous fury here, which may come as a surprise after your stint on the sheltered forest trail.

A spur trail leads down the cliffs to the beach; it's worth hiking during low tide when you can crawl through the tunnel of Arch Rock and explore the beach. Many visitors are content to stay on top of Arch Rock and enjoy the view of the surging waters below. If luck is with you, you'll catch sight of a passing gray whale, or at least a couple of sea lions.

For more information, contact Point Reyes National Seashore, 415/464-5100, www.nps.gov/pore.

Options

Although there is no way to extend the biking part of this bike-and-hike trip, you can extend the hike by backtracking 0.25 mile from Arch Rock to a junction with Coast Trail. Turn left (north) on Coast Trail and follow it for 1 mile to the left turnoff for Kelham Beach, which is unsigned but marked by a single massive eucalyptus tree. Or, you can hike a 4-mile loop and return to the bike rack by following Coast Trail north for 0.5 mile, turning right on Sky Trail, then right again on Baldy Trail.

Driving Directions

From San Francisco, cross the Golden Gate Bridge and drive north on U.S. 101 for 7.5 miles. Take the Sir Francis Drake Boulevard exit west toward San Anselmo and drive 20 miles to the town of Olema. At Olema, turn right (north) on Highway 1 for about 150 yards, then turn left on Bear Valley Road. Drive 0.5 mile, then turn left at the sign for Seashore Headquarters Information. Drive 0.25 mile and park in the large lot on the left, past the visitor center. Start riding along the park road, heading for the signed Bear Valley Trail.

Route Directions

0.0 Park at Bear Valley Trailhead just past the visitor center. Ride west on the continuation of the park road, which turns to dirt at a wide gate. *Supplies are available less than a mile away in Olema; water is available at the visitor center.*

1.6 Divide Meadow.

3.1 Bike rack and junction with Glen, Baldy, and Bear Valley Trails; TURN AROUND. *Lock up your bike and hike 0.9 mile on Bear Valley Trail to Arch Rock (straight ahead).*

6.2 Arrive at starting point.

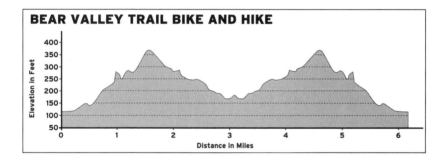

5 POINT REYES LIGHTHOUSE   BEST ◖

Point Reyes National Seashore

PAVED ROADS WITH MODERATE CAR TRAFFIC

Difficulty: 3 (4 if windy)   **Total Distance:** 45 miles (or 20-mile option)

Riding Time: 3.5-4.5 hours   **Elevation Gain:** 1,900 feet

Summary: An often windswept cruise through the rural Point Reyes countryside, this route offers optional stops at a few of the park's highlights.

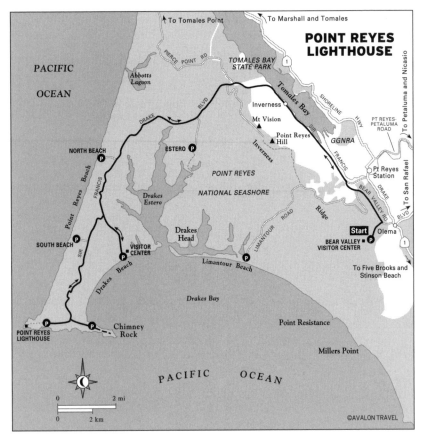

Road cycling in Point Reyes National Seashore can be heavenly if the weather gods are on your side. If they aren't, you could face headwinds of 40-plus miles per hour, or fog so dense you miss all the scenery the park has to offer. Remember this: Autumn and spring days are the surest bets for clear weather. Winter isn't bad

© ANN MARIE BROWN

A visit to the lighthouse is one highlight of a road ride in Point Reyes.

either, and that's when you have the best chance of spotting migrating whales from the park's shores. This road tour travels to two of the park's best whale-watching spots—the Point Reyes Lighthouse and Chimney Rock—and detours to gastronomic delights at Drakes Beach Café (a lunch of seasonal greens and barbecued oysters) and Drakes Bay Family Farms (fresh oysters straight from the shell).

From the Bear Valley Visitor Center, the route follows Bear Valley Road to Sir Francis Drake Highway and the bayside town of Inverness. Then Sir Francis Drake heads northwest into the park, leaving most of civilization behind with a short but steep ascent up and over Inverness Ridge. The ride continues on Sir Francis Drake as it threads through fields of colorful wild mustard and acres of cow pastures to the western tip of Point Reyes National Seashore.

At Chimney Rock Trailhead, you can walk a 1.5-mile stretch where more than 60 species of wildflowers bloom in springtime on a narrow, windswept headland jutting into Drakes Bay, or look for elephant seals and gray whales in winter or spring. The ride finishes at Point Reyes Lighthouse, where 300-plus steps descend to this breathtaking coastal promontory. To tour the lighthouse, plan your trip for Thursday through Monday; it's closed year-round on Tuesday and Wednesday.

For more information, contact Point Reyes National Seashore, 415/464-5100, www.nps.gov/pore. Drakes Beach Café (415/669-1297, www.drakescafe.com) is located at 1 Drakes Beach Road. Drakes Bay Family Farms (415/669-1149, www.drakesbayoyster.com) is located at 17171 Sir Francis Drake Boulevard. Hours vary seasonally.

Options

If the wind is too stiff to make this ride enjoyable, try this more protected option: Begin your ride as described, then bear right at mile 7.4 on Pierce Point Road. Pedal 1.2 miles and then turn right on Tomales Bay State Park Road. One mile down the park road is lovely Heart's Desire Beach. An out-and-back ride to this mostly wind-sheltered beach is about 20 miles.

Driving Directions

From San Francisco, cross the Golden Gate Bridge and drive north on U.S. 101 for 7.5 miles. Take the Sir Francis Drake Boulevard exit west toward San Anselmo and drive 20 miles to the town of Olema. At Olema, turn right (north) on Highway 1 for about 150 yards, then turn left on Bear Valley Road. Drive 0.5 mile, then turn left at the sign for Seashore Headquarters Information. Drive 0.25 mile and park by the visitor center.

Route Directions

0.0 Park at Bear Valley Visitor Center, then ride back out the park road the way you came in. *Water is available at the visitor center.*

0.2 LEFT on Bear Valley Road.

1.8 LEFT on Sir Francis Drake Highway.

5.9 Town of Inverness. *Supplies are available.*

7.4 LEFT at Y-junction with Pierce Point Road.

8.7 STRAIGHT at junction with Mount Vision Road.

9.4 STRAIGHT at junction with Estero Trailhead Road.

10.4 Drakes Bay Family Farms entrance on left. *If the oyster company is open, stop in for a grown-in-Point Reyes snack.*

13.2 STRAIGHT at junction for North Beach.

15.1 RIGHT at junction with Kenneth C. Patrick Visitor Center and Drakes Beach (save the left fork for your return trip).

19.4 LEFT at access road for Chimney Rock Trailhead.

20.3 Chimney Rock Trailhead. TURN AROUND. *Hike or mountain bike the 1.5-mile Chimney Rock Trail in winter for whale-watching and in spring for wildflowers. From December to April, walk a few hundred yards to the Elephant Seal Overlook to see the seals hauled out on Drakes Beach.*

21.2 LEFT on Sir Francis Drake Highway.

21.8 Point Reyes Lighthouse parking lot. TURN AROUND. *Tour the lighthouse and neighboring visitor center.*

26.7 RIGHT for Kenneth C. Patrick Visitor Center and Drakes Beach.

28.3 Drake's Beach parking lot. TURN AROUND. *The visitor center features fascinating exhibits on local history, flora, and fauna (open weekends only). Drakes Beach Café serves lunch Friday–Monday in winter, Thursday–Monday in spring and summer, and Saturday–Sunday in autumn.*

29.9 RIGHT on Sir Francis Drake Highway.

45.0 Arrive at starting point.

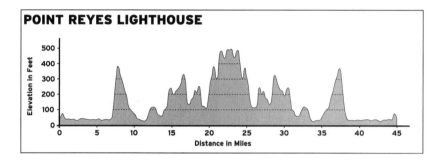

POINT REYES LIGHTHOUSE

6 STEWART TRAIL
Point Reyes National Seashore

DIRT ROAD

Difficulty: 4   **Total Distance:** 13 miles

Riding Time: 2-3 hours   **Elevation Gain:** 2,500 feet

Summary: An up-and-down ride on a conifer-lined dirt road leads from the inland valley to the Point Reyes coast.

Few national parks permit bikes on their trails, and even fewer allow bike-in camping at remote campgrounds. Point Reyes National Seashore is a rare exception, and Stewart Trail from Five Brooks Trailhead is your ticket to two backcountry camps in Point Reyes: Glen and Wildcat. Those wishing to bike-backpack can make a reservation and get a permit for one of the camps. Riders looking for a challenging day-time sojourn will also enjoy pedaling Stewart Trail.

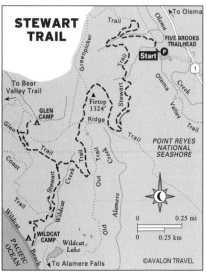

Be prepared for some climbing; this is an aerobically strenuous ride with a long ascent in both directions of the out-and-back. The initial climb begins 0.25 mile from the parking lot and makes a steady 1,200-foot ascent over 3.5 miles to a ridge called Fir Top. The name is apt; the area is completely shaded by Douglas firs. Then Stewart Trail drops steeply toward the ocean, losing all that hard-won elevation, plus another 100 feet. At 5.2 miles is the turnoff for forest-sheltered Glen Camp, where some riders spend the night. Stewart Trail continues downhill to the coast and Wildcat Camp. As you descend, be sure to give your brakes a rest now and then by stopping to enjoy occasional peeks at the ocean through the trees. And keep in mind that you'll face this slope in the uphill direction on your way home. Stewart Trail ends 6.5 miles out at Wildcat Camp. Day visitors and campers alike will want to lock up their wheels and head to the neighboring beach to explore.

For more information and/or camping permits, contact Point Reyes National Seashore, 415/464-5100, www.nps.gov/pore.

Stewart Trail provides a challenging day trip or the chance for an overnight camping experience in one of two backcountry camps in Point Reyes.

Options

If you're burning with energy, an option from Wildcat Camp is to hike two miles south on Coast Trail (bikes are not allowed) to visit Alamere Falls, one of the Bay Area's loveliest waterfalls. The falls drop 50 feet over a coastal bluff to the sea.

Driving Directions

From San Francisco, cross the Golden Gate Bridge and drive north on U.S. 101 for 7.5 miles. Take the Sir Francis Drake Boulevard exit west toward San Anselmo and drive 20 miles to the town of Olema. At Olema, turn left (south) on Highway 1 for 3.5 miles to Five Brooks Trailhead on the right.

Route Directions

0.0 Park at Five Brooks Trailhead. Ride out the paved road past a large pond. *Supplies are available in Olema; water is available at the trailhead.*

0.2 RIGHT on wide Stewart Trail.

3.0 RIGHT to stay on Stewart Trail at junction with Ridge Trail.

3.8 Arrive at Fir Top summit at 1,324 feet.

5.2 LEFT to stay on Stewart Trail at junction with Glen Trail (campers staying at Glen Camp turn right here).

6.5 Arrive at Wildcat Camp; TURN AROUND. *Lock up your bike and*

*visit neighboring Wildcat Beach, or take a two-mile hike south on the
Coast Trail to Alamere Falls.*

13.0 Arrive at starting point.

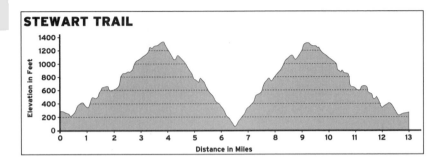

7 BOLINAS RIDGE AND OLEMA VALLEY LOOP

Golden Gate National Recreation Area near Olema

DIRT ROAD

Difficulty: 2   **Total Distance:** 15 miles (or 26-mile option)

Riding Time: 2 hours   **Elevation Gain:** 1,000 feet

Summary: Pedal uphill past the bovines and through the grasslands of Bolinas Ridge, then choose from a variety of fast and fun descents.

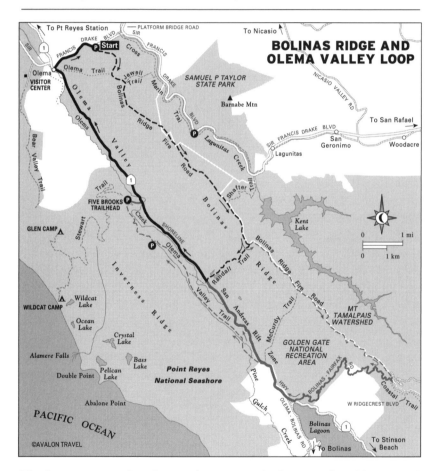

The first time you ride Bolinas Ridge, you wonder how a trail could go up and down so much without ever leveling out. The path seems to have no pedal-and-cruise sections; you are either climbing up or coasting down the whole way (more of the latter than the former). The ridge's roller-coaster grassland terrain is just

Open pasturelands line the northern edge of Bolinas Ridge near Olema.

plain fun, and scenic to boot: Its high points afford expansive views of Bolinas Lagoon to the south and Tomales Bay to the north. The trail is well suited for all levels of riders; beginners can go out and back for a few miles while the more advanced can choose from a variety of loops.

The key is to start on the Olema side of Bolinas Ridge at the Sir Francis Drake Boulevard trailhead, rather than on the Mount Tamalpais side at the Bolinas–Fairfax Road trailhead. From the Olema side, less ambitious riders can pedal southward for a handful of miles as the trail climbs moderately. Much of Bolinas Ridge is cattle country, so you'll have to lift your bike over several livestock gates in the first couple miles of trail. Be sure to leave every gate the way you found it, either open or closed. The route carves through open pasturelands until the 5.4-mile mark, where it suddenly enters a thick of Douglas fir and redwood forest. Say good-bye to the sun and the views and hello to the refreshing woods. When you've had enough and are ready to turn around and head home, a fun descent awaits.

Meanwhile, those with more energy can continue southeast on Bolinas Ridge and then loop around to Highway 1 on Randall Trail, a steep downhill track. The second half of the loop is an easy cruise northward on mostly level Highway 1 back to Olema. Your car awaits one mile up Sir Francis Drake Boulevard. If the idea of riding on pavement insults your mountain biking sensibilities, you can omit a few road miles by riding the dirt Olema Valley Trail, which parallels Highway 1 all the way from Dogtown to the Five Brooks Trailhead. This is a dry-season option only, however; marshy Olema Valley is notorious for flooding with even the slightest rain.

For more information, contact Golden Gate National Recreation Area, 415/331-1540, www.nps.gov/goga.

Options

If you're enjoying Bolinas Ridge Trail so much that you are not ready to loop back when you reach Randall Trail at 6.2 miles out, you can sign up for a much longer and harder day by continuing an additional 3.2 miles to the high point of Bolinas Ridge at 1,700 feet, then pedaling 1.7 miles farther to a junction with paved Bolinas–Fairfax Road. A right turn here will provide you with a fast and furious descent over 4.5 miles to Highway 1, where you turn right and ride 10 miles back to your car on Sir Francis Drake Boulevard just outside of Olema. This is a ride worthy of bragging rights, totaling 26 miles and 2,200 feet of elevation gain.

Driving Directions

From San Francisco, cross the Golden Gate Bridge on U.S. 101 and travel north toward San Rafael. Take the Sir Francis Drake Boulevard exit west toward San Anselmo and drive 19.5 miles to the trailhead for the Bolinas Ridge Trail on the left side of the road. If you reach the town of Olema and Highway 1, you've gone 1 mile too far.

Route Directions

0.0 Park at the Bolinas Ridge trailhead pullout alongside Sir Francis Drake Boulevard, one mile northeast of Olema. Ride uphill and veer left onto the wide dirt road. *Supplies are available in Olema.*

1.4 RIGHT at junction with Jewell Trail to stay on Bolinas Ridge.

5.2 STRAIGHT at junction with Shafter Trail.

6.2 RIGHT at junction with Randall Trail.

7.9 RIGHT at junction with Highway 1.

14.0 RIGHT at junction with Sir Francis Drake Boulevard in Olema.

15.0 Arrive at starting point.

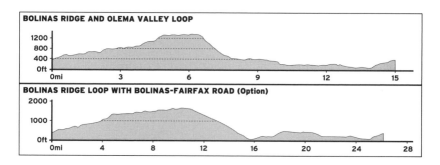

8 CROSS MARIN TRAIL AND BOLINAS RIDGE LOOP

Samuel P. Taylor State Park near Olema

DIRT ROAD/TRAIL AND PAVED BIKE PATH

Difficulty: 3

Riding Time: 2.5 hours

Total Distance: 13.4 miles

Elevation Gain: 1,250 feet

Summary: An old railroad trail leads into the redwoods for an easy ride, but ambitious mountain bikers can follow a strenuous loop back to their starting point.

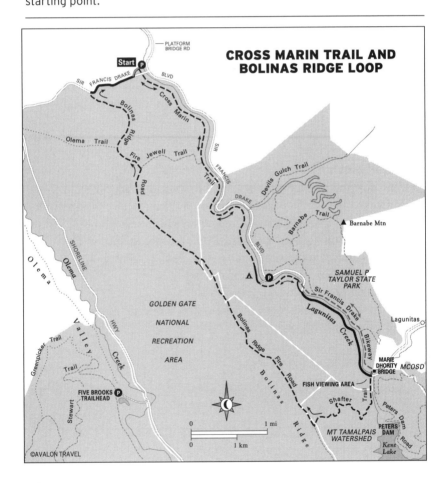

A cyclist and his dog enjoy the redwood-shaded Cross Marin Trail.

The Cross Marin Trail/Sir Francis Drake Bikeway is one trail with two names, under two different park jurisdictions. It's called the Cross Marin Trail when it's on Golden Gate National Recreation Area land, and the Sir Francis Drake Bikeway when it's on Samuel P. Taylor State Park land. The trail with two names is an old rail trail, built in 1874 by the North Pacific Coast Railroad. It offers something for skinny tires and fat tires alike, with three miles of smooth pavement and another two miles of gravel and dirt suitable for mountain bikes. While plenty of people ride out and back on the bike path only, a more strenuous loop can be made by connecting to Bolinas Ridge Trail.

The route begins in dense woods as it travels parallel to Lagunitas Creek, also called Papermill Creek. This is mellow pedaling on smooth pavement; the first few miles are suitable even for young children. There's plenty of time to look around and admire the thick second-growth redwood stands, which are cushioned by an undergrowth of sorrel, ferns, and flowering blue milkmaids in spring. Too soon, your primeval redwood fantasy gets rudely interrupted by campgrounds, restrooms, and other indicators of civilization. Just beyond Redwood Grove Picnic Area, the paved surface erodes to gravel and dirt, and skinny tires must turn around. Mountain bikers continue riding, crossing a footbridge (an old railroad trestle) over Sir Francis Drake Boulevard. Two miles later the trail reaches the park boundary, where Shafter Bridge arches over Lagunitas Creek. Here, novice riders should turn around and head back the way they came; more energetic bikers should continue onward. In years past, riders had to ford the stream here to access the trails on the other side, but in 2004 the Marie Dhority Bridge was built to accommodate bikers and pedestrians, and to protect the spawning steelhead trout that make their way up this stream in the rainy season. As you ride over this sturdy bridge, note the rock-lined pools in the creek below; in summer this is a popular swimming area known as The Inkwells.

Now comes the only treacherous part of this ride: You must cross Sir Francis Drake Boulevard with great caution (it's best to walk your bike) and then make your way to the parking lot to your right, on the far (northwest) side of the creek. At the parking lot, pick up Shafter Fire Road and prepare for a gnarly, 1.8-mile winding climb that slays even the best of 'em (1,100-foot gain). At the top, a heavenly, mostly downhill cruise on Bolinas Ridge Trail awaits. Where the trail ends at Sir Francis Drake Highway, cruise down the paved road back to your car.

For more information, contact Golden Gate National Recreation Area, 415/331-1540, www.nps.gov/goga; or Samuel P. Taylor State Park, 415/488-9897, www.parks.ca.gov.

Driving Directions

From San Francisco, cross the Golden Gate Bridge on U.S. 101 and drive north for 7.5 miles. Take the Sir Francis Drake Boulevard exit west toward San Anselmo and drive 18.7 miles to the right turnoff for Platform Bridge Road, located 3.4 miles past the main entrance to Samuel P. Taylor State Park. (If you reach the town of Olema and Highway 1, you have gone 1.8 miles too far.) Turn right on Platform Bridge Road and park in the pullout on the left.

Route Directions

0.0 Park at the Platform Bridge Road trailhead. Ride on the paved path leading from the pullout, cross a concrete bridge, go about 50 feet, then turn left on the signed Cross Marin Trail. *Supplies are available in Olema, two miles west.*

1.5 STRAIGHT at junction with Jewell Trail.

2.7 State park camping and picnic areas. *Water is available.*

3.0 Pavement ends; skinny tires must turn around.

3.4 Cross bridge over Sir Francis Drake Highway.

5.0 Trail reaches Marie Dhority Bridge over Lagunitas Creek's Inkwells. Cross the bridge and then walk your bike across Sir Francis Drake Boulevard and 30 yards northwest, to the parking area on the far (northwest) side of the creek.

5.2 Take Shafter Fire Road uphill.

7.0 RIGHT on Bolinas Ridge Trail at end of climb.

12.2 RIGHT on paved Sir Francis Drake Highway at end of Bolinas
   Ridge Trail.
13.3 LEFT on Platform Bridge Road.
13.4 Arrive at starting point.

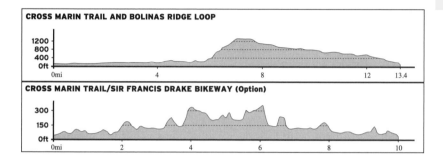

9 NICASIO RESERVOIR LOOP
western Marin County

PAVED ROADS WITH MODERATE CAR TRAFFIC

Difficulty: 2   **Total Distance:** 24.5 miles (or 44-mile option)

Riding Time: 2 hours   **Elevation Gain:** 900 feet

Summary: The country roads of western Marin County make up the backbone of this gentle, scenic ride.

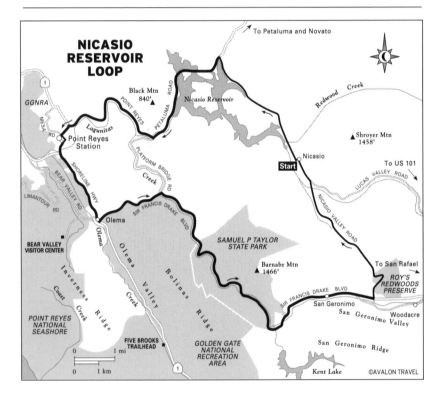

A favorite of Marin County cyclists, this 24.5-mile road ride is an easy-to-moderate loop on mostly level back roads surrounding the small town of Nicasio and its large reservoir. Although these roads see some traffic, especially on nice-weather weekends, most drivers in the area are accustomed to sharing the road with bikes.

The loop begins in Nicasio, a gentrified country town—the kind of place where almost everybody owns at least one horse. The first 10 miles on Nicasio Valley Road and Point Reyes–Petaluma Road provide nearly perfect cycling, with a wide shoulder, smooth paved surface, and relatively few cars. The two roads skirt the

The scenic back roads of the Nicasio Reservoir Loop are favored by Marin County cyclists.

edge of Nicasio Reservoir, a surprisingly large and pretty lake that is popular year-round for shoreline bass fishing.

Upon reaching Highway 1, you'll ride through Point Reyes Station and Olema—both good stops for coffee, food, and camaraderie with other bikers. Then Sir Francis Drake Boulevard climbs and curves through Samuel P. Taylor State Park and continues gently uphill through a succession of small towns: Lagunitas, Forest Knolls, and San Geronimo. There's more traffic on this second half of the loop, but it's still manageable. By the golf course in San Geronimo, you'll turn north on Nicasio Valley Road, where there's a lovely grove of redwoods known as Roy's Redwoods, a perfect place to get off the saddle for a short walk. All in all, this is an easy, low-pressure ride, with plenty of places to stop and enjoy the countryside.

Options
You could easily add on up to 10 miles each way by parking near the junction of Lucas Valley Road and U.S. 101, then riding your bike to Nicasio. (To do so, leave your car on one of the side streets that intersects Lucas Valley Road. The road has a wide shoulder for the first 4 miles, then no shoulder at all for the next 6, but not a lot of traffic, either.)

Driving Directions
From San Rafael, drive 3 miles north on U.S. 101 and take the Lucas Valley Road

exit. Drive 10.4 miles west on Lucas Valley Road, then turn right on Nicasio Valley Road. Drive 0.5 mile and park in the town of Nicasio.

Route Directions

0.0 Park in the town of Nicasio and ride north on Nicasio Valley Road. *Supplies are available in Nicasio or San Rafael.*

3.2 LEFT on Point Reyes–Petaluma Road.

6.3 RIGHT to stay on Point Reyes–Petaluma Road.

9.4 LEFT on Shoreline Highway (Highway 1).

9.8 LEFT on Shoreline Highway through town of Point Reyes Station. *Supplies are available in Point Reyes Station.*

10.0 RIGHT to get back on Highway 1.

10.2 STRAIGHT to stay on Highway 1.

12.2 LEFT on Sir Francis Drake Boulevard in Olema. *Supplies are available in Olema.*

17.0 Pass through Samuel P. Taylor State Park.

20.0 LEFT on Nicasio Valley Road by San Geronimo golf course. *Roy's Redwoods Open Space Preserve makes a nice place for a short walk.*

24.5 Arrive at starting point.

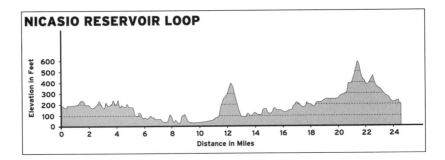

10 PINE MOUNTAIN LOOP
Marin Municipal Water District near Fairfax

DIRT ROAD

Difficulty: 3

Riding Time: 2.5 hours

Total Distance: 13.2 miles

Elevation Gain: 2,000 feet

Summary: Pedal a challenging mountain-biking loop that travels through the wild landscape of the Marin Watershed.

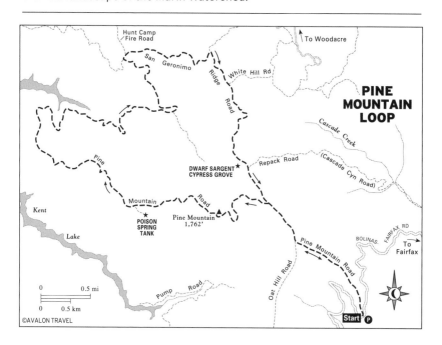

The heart and soul of Marin mountain biking lies in the lands west of Fairfax, where the crowded county suburbs give way to grasslands, open ridges, and mixed woodlands of oak, bay, and Douglas fir. The first mile of the Pine Mountain Loop gives you long looks over your right shoulder of the civilization you are leaving behind—much of Marin County, San Pablo Bay, the Richmond Bridge, and Mount Diablo are in plain view—but soon you will see only chaparral-lined hillsides and rolling ridgetops.

The summit of Pine Mountain, elevation 1,762, forms the first challenge in this loop's advanced aerobic workout. You'll climb 700 feet to the top, often on a rutted and rocky surface, in this loop's first 2.3 miles. The next 4 miles are much easier; most of your energy will be spent controlling your speed on swift descents.

A few healthy climbs provide an aerobic workout on the Pine Mountain Loop near Fairfax.

A short but lovely section meanders along the edge of Kent Lake. Then at 7.2 miles you'll start to climb again, this time gaining 1,100 feet spaced out over 4 miles. Gear down and suck in as much oxygen as you can.

An unusual sight worth noting is a stand of dwarf Sargent cypress trees off San Geronimo Ridge Fire Road. The Sargent cypress is a rare evergreen that grows in scattered groves in the region surrounding Mount Tamalpais. It is usually stunted in size when rooted in serpentine soil, as is the case here. Cypress trees that are more than 100 years old may be only a few feet tall. Watch for the miniature Sargent cypress forest between miles 10.5 and 11.

For more information on Marin Municipal Water District lands, phone Sky Oaks Ranger Station at 415/945-1181 or visit www.marinwater.org.

Options

If you are riding in the winter or spring months, you could add a short bike-and-hike adventure to this ride. After the initial 1.1-mile climb on Pine Mountain Road, turn left on Oat Hill Road and ride downhill. In 0.3 mile, you'll see a large trail signboard on the right. Bikes aren't allowed on this lovely path, so lock up and/or stash your bike, then hike downhill for 0.7 mile to the top of Carson Falls, one of Marin County's prettiest waterfalls. It's a long chain of four pool-and-drop cataracts that pour into rock-lined pools. Carson Falls' green-gray rock looks like serpentine, but it's actually a type of greenstone basalt. Tread carefully near the water's edge; not only is the wet rock slippery, but the pools are also home to threatened amphibians, including the foothill yellow-legged frog.

Driving Directions

From San Francisco, cross the Golden Gate Bridge and drive north on U.S. 101 for 7.5 miles. Take the Sir Francis Drake Boulevard exit west toward San Anselmo, then drive 6 miles to the town of Fairfax. Turn left by the Fairfax sign (on Pacheco Road), then turn right immediately on Broadway. In one block, turn left on Bolinas Road. Drive 3.8 miles on Bolinas Road, past the golf course, to the dirt parking area on the left side of the road.

Route Directions

0.0 Park in the dirt parking area on the left side of Bolinas–Fairfax Road. The fire road begins across the road. *Supplies are available in Fairfax.*

1.1 STRAIGHT at junction with Oat Hill Road. *Or turn left for a bike-and-hike trip to Carson Falls; see* Options.

1.5 LEFT to stay on Pine Mountain Road.

2.3 Summit of Pine Mountain at 1,762 feet.

5.6 RIGHT at junction near Kent Lake.

8.8 RIGHT at four-way intersection.

9.8 RIGHT on San Geronimo Ridge Fire Road.

11.2 RIGHT at junction with Repack Trail (also called Cascade Canyon) on left.

11.7 STRAIGHT to rejoin Pine Mountain Road.

12.1 STRAIGHT at junction with Oat Hill Road.

13.2 Arrive at starting point.

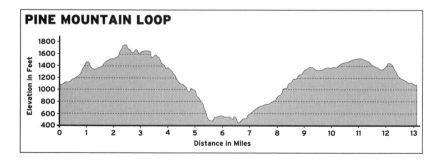

11 TAMARANCHO LOOP BEST 🄲
Tamarancho Boy Scout Camp near Fairfax

DIRT SINGLE-TRACK

Difficulty: 3   **Total Distance:** 11.7 miles

Riding Time: 2 hours   **Elevation Gain:** 1,000 feet

Summary: Mountain bikers find single-track nirvana on this loop near the town of Fairfax.

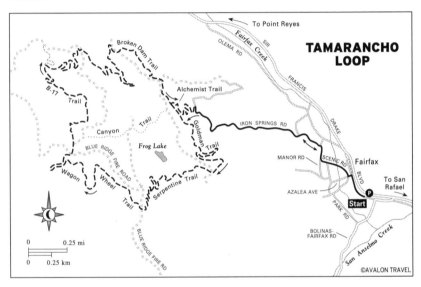

It costs five bucks to get a day-use permit to ride your mountain bike at the Boy Scouts' Camp Tamarancho, but think of it as a pass to the best mountain bike park around. If you live near Fairfax, invest in the annual pass (about $50) and you'll have long-term access to gorgeous single-track that was built by mountain bikers for mountain bikers. Whether you come here repeatedly or only one day, with your first glimpse of the sign that says "Bicycles MUST stay on single-track," you will think you have died and gone to mountain biking heaven.

Tamarancho is deservedly popular, so the trails can be crowded on weekends. Your best bet is to ride here on a weekday, and preferably not at midafternoon in summer, when it can be hot as Hades. There are no trail choices to make, just a single loop set up for mountain bikers. Yes, it's almost exclusively single-track, and yes again, the loop presents plenty of technical challenges. Beginning riders probably would not be happy here. Some hikers also use the trail, although most pedestrians stick to the camp's dirt roads on the inside of this loop, where bikes are not permitted.

The Tamarancho Loop rolls and dips, curving in and out of dense oak and bay woodland and open, grassy areas. Several short climbs of less than a mile in length give you a moderate workout, but without the drudgery of a long, sustained ascent. You'll snake through more than three dozen switchbacks along the route. It's all fun, but make sure your eyes and ears are alert for other riders, because otherwise you may not see them until you're right on top of them.

One leg of the loop, Wagon Wheel Trail, leaves the Boy Scouts' property and travels through Marin County Open Space land. The entire route is well signed (always watch for the arrow signs where the single-track crosses fire roads). Although the loop itself is just over 7 miles, the entire ride length is 11.7 miles because there is no parking permitted anywhere near Tamarancho. You leave your car in downtown Fairfax and ride 1.6 miles to a connecting trail off pothole-ridden Iron Springs Road, which deposits you on the loop. The loop itself can be ridden in either direction; a clockwise loop is described here.

For more information, contact the Boy Scouts' Camp Tamarancho, 415/454-1081, www.boyscouts-marin.org.

Driving Directions

From San Francisco, cross the Golden Gate Bridge and drive north on U.S. 101 for 7.5 miles. Take the Sir Francis Drake Boulevard exit west toward San Anselmo, then drive 6 miles to the town of Fairfax. Turn left by the Fairfax sign on Pacheco Road, then turn right on Broadway and park in downtown Fairfax. The public parking lot on your right (bordered by Pacheco Road, Sir Francis Drake Boulevard, and Broadway) allows free four-hour parking.

Route Directions

0.0 Park in downtown Fairfax in the four-hour parking lot between Sir Francis Drake Boulevard and Broadway. Exit the parking lot and ride west on Broadway. *Supplies are available in downtown Fairfax.*

0.3 LEFT on Azalea (west of Fairfax Lumber), then immediate RIGHT on Scenic.

0.5 RIGHT on Manor.

0.6 LEFT on Rockridge.

0.7 STRAIGHT on Iron Springs Road (Rockridge veers to the right). Watch for large potholes on Iron Springs Road.

1.6 LEFT on single-track connector trail to Tamarancho (Alchemist Trail).

2.2 LEFT on Goldman Trail.

2.9 Cross fire road to join Serpentine Trail.

4.0 Cross fire road to join Wagon Wheel Trail.

5.5 STRAIGHT on fire road to connect to B-17 Trail on left; steep hill.

6.9 RIGHT on Broken Dam Trail at junction with B-17 Extension Trail.

9.1 Cross Iron Springs Road to join Goldman Trail.

9.5 LEFT on single-track leading back to Iron Springs Road.

10.1 RIGHT on Iron Springs Road.

11.7 Retrace route through Fairfax to arrive at starting point.

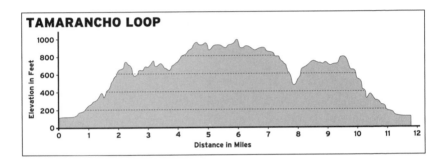

12 FAIRFAX AND MOUNT TAMALPAIS LOOP
Bolinas-Fairfax Road to Mount Tamalpais

PAVED ROADS WITH MODERATE CAR TRAFFIC

Difficulty: 3

Total Distance: 31.8 miles

Riding Time: 3-4 hours

Elevation Gain: 2,200 feet

Summary: A classic tour of Mount Tamalpais and the Marin Watershed, this route is suitable for experienced road cyclists.

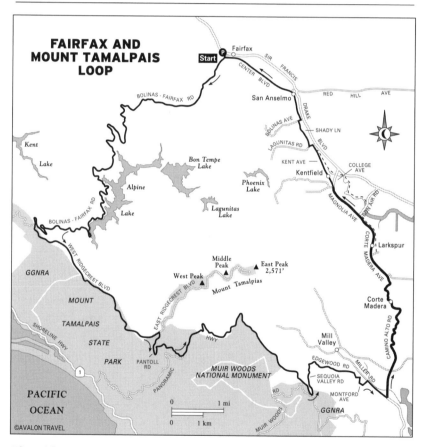

If you like country back roads with few cars and a variety of scenic terrain, you'll love riding Bolinas–Fairfax Road. This 32-mile loop travels the rolling upper portion of the old stage road from the town of Fairfax to the top of Bolinas Ridge. (The steeper lower stretch of Bolinas–Fairfax Road is ridden in the *Stinson Beach and Mount Tamalpais Loop*, ride 15.) The winding pavement curves through miles of open space in the protected lands of the Marin Watershed, where deer and raptors are more common than people, and cyclists are more common than automobiles. Most of the route travels through open grasslands and can be quite warm in the summer months, but the scenery changes dramatically at about 7 miles, when you reach the western lakeshore of large Alpine Lake, then cross its dam and enter dense redwood forest for a heart-pumping, 2.5-mile climb to Bolinas Ridge (850-foot gain).

At the road's high point, you'll turn left and pedal along one of the Bay Area's most filmed and photographed roads—West Ridgecrest Boulevard, site of dozens of car commercials and calendar shots. Ocean views are dazzling from this high ridge, which is surrounded by the grassy hillsides of Mount Tamalpais State Park. You'll gain another 500 feet as you traverse the ridge, then make a fast descent down Pantoll Road to Panoramic Highway. A left turn here brings you to Four Corners (exercise caution on this no-shoulder stretch of narrow pavement), where you make a transitional descent from the open ridgeline roads of Mount Tamalpais to the narrow hillside streets of Mill Valley. It's down, down, down for a solid eight miles from the top of Pantoll Road on Mount Tam to Miller Avenue in Mill Valley. Your brakes will get plenty of work.

The final nine miles of the loop are a northward run through the Marin County towns of Corte Madera, Larkspur, Kentfield, Ross, and San Anselmo. A lunch stop at one of the cafés in downtown Larkspur is highly recommended.

Driving Directions

From San Francisco, cross the Golden Gate Bridge and drive north on U.S. 101 for 7.5 miles. Take the Sir Francis Drake Boulevard exit west toward San Anselmo, then drive 6 miles to the town of Fairfax. Turn left by the Fairfax sign on Pacheco Road, then turn right on Broadway and park in downtown Fairfax. The public parking lot on your right (bordered by Pacheco Road, Sir Francis Drake Boulevard, and Broadway) allows free four-hour parking.

Route Directions

0.0 Park in downtown Fairfax in the four-hour parking lot between Sir Francis Drake Boulevard and Broadway. Exit the parking lot and ride west on Broadway for one block to the start of Bolinas–Fairfax Road. *Supplies are available in downtown Fairfax.*

0.1 LEFT on Bolinas–Fairfax Road (note that this road is sometimes signed as Bolinas Road or Fairfax–Bolinas Road).

7.9 Cross Alpine Dam and begin steep climb through shady redwood forest.

10.4 LEFT on West Ridgecrest Boulevard at top of Bolinas Ridge.

14.3 RIGHT on Pantoll Road; begin fast descent.

15.7 LEFT on Panoramic Highway.

20.2 LEFT on Sequoia Valley Road at Four Corners junction (Sequoia Valley Road changes names to Edgewood Road and then Molino Avenue).

22.0 LEFT on Montford Avenue.

22.1 LEFT to stay on Montford Avenue.

22.3 RIGHT on Miller Avenue. *Supplies are available on Miller Avenue.*

22.7 LEFT on Camino Alto by Tamalpais High School.

23.2 Cross East Blithedale Avenue to stay on Camino Alto (Camino Alto changes names to Corte Madera Avenue and then Magnolia Avenue). *Cafés, restaurants, and supplies are available on Magnolia Avenue in Larkspur.*

26.7 Larkspur bike path runs alongside road; follow path or road.

27.1 Cross Bon Air Road; bike path ends; follow bike lane.

27.9 LEFT on Kent Avenue, which becomes Poplar Avenue.

28.8 LEFT on Lagunitas Road at Ross Commons Park.

28.9 RIGHT on Shady Lane.

29.6 RIGHT on Bolinas Avenue, then immediate LEFT on San Anselmo Avenue.

30.2 Follow Bridge Avenue, then LEFT on Sycamore Avenue (Sycamore changes names to Center Boulevard, Lansdale Avenue, then back to Center Boulevard).

31.8 Arrive at starting point.

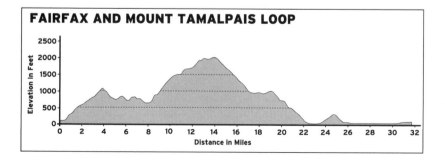

FAIRFAX AND MOUNT TAMALPAIS LOOP

13 CHINA CAMP BAY VIEW LOOP BEST ☾
China Camp State Park near San Rafael

DIRT ROAD AND SINGLE-TRACK

Difficulty: 3 | **Total Distance:** 11.6 miles
Riding Time: 2 hours | **Elevation Gain:** 600 feet

Summary: Enjoy fun single-track riding in one of Marin County's most popular biking parks, and a glimpse at San Pablo Bay's shrimp-fishing history.

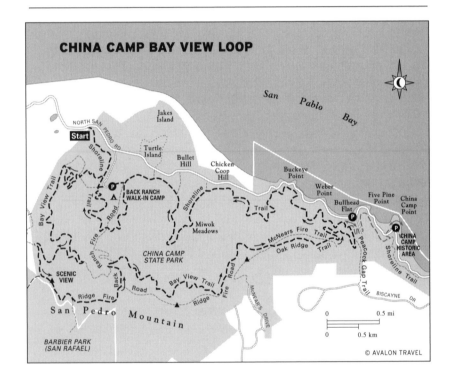

China Camp State Park is a rare bird in the California State Park system. One of only a handful of state parks that allows mountain bikes on single-track trails, China Camp also holds a scenic location on San Pablo Bay, with blue-water vistas from more than 1,500 shoreline acres. Bikers and hikers generally mind their manners and get along just fine here, although in recent years the park has seen a lot more of the former and fewer of the latter, especially on weekends. Over time, China Camp has metamorphosed into a biker's park.

It's also a historic preserve, showcasing the remains of a Chinese shrimp-fishing

Views of San Pablo Bay can be seen from China Camp's trails.

village from the 19th century, where immigrants netted shrimp from the bay. Don't neglect visiting the historic buildings and experiencing the unique history of this area.

Several rides are possible at China Camp. Beginners should stick to the smooth single-track Shoreline Trail (see *Options*), while more advanced riders will want to tackle the rutted, steep hills in the backcountry of the park. The route described here is a good workout that supplies plenty of short but steep grades for practicing your ascending and descending skills. Highlights include a visit to one of Marin County's best viewpoints, a Nike radar site at 900 feet above the bay; and pedaling on Oak Ridge Trail, a lovely pathway through grasslands and oak woodlands.

For more information, contact China Camp State Park, 415/456-0766, www.parks.ca.gov.

Options

Novices should begin their love affair with China Camp State Park's trails with an easy cruise on Shoreline Trail. Pick up the single-track by the park entrance kiosk and stay on it all the way to Miwok Meadows Group Camp (2.6 miles), where you follow a dirt road for a short distance before getting back on Shoreline Trail. At 5.2 miles, go left on Village Trail, then cross San Pedro Road and follow the pavement to China Camp Village. Here you can lock up your bike and explore the historic buildings and museum. A snack bar is open on weekends and holidays. An out-and-back ride to the old fishing village covers 11.2 miles, but you can shorten your trip to 8 miles by returning on North San Pedro Road.

Driving Directions

From San Francisco, cross the Golden Gate Bridge and drive north on U.S. 101

for 11 miles to San Rafael. Take the North San Pedro exit and drive east for 3.5 miles to China Camp State Park.

Route Directions

0.0 Park along the road near Back Ranch Meadows Campground. Follow Shoreline Trail from the right side of the kiosk. *Supplies are available in San Rafael. Water is available at the campground.*

0.1 RIGHT on Bay View Trail.

0.5 RIGHT on fire road, then immediate LEFT back on Bay View Trail.

1.1 LEFT to stay on Bay View Trail.

2.0 RIGHT (hairpin) on trail to Bay Hills Drive.

2.6 LEFT on paved Bay Hills Drive; steep uphill.

3.0 Nike radar base; great views of Marin County and San Francisco Bay.

3.3 LEFT on Ridge Fire Road.

3.6 LEFT at junction; steep downhill.

3.9 RIGHT on fire road at power line junction; stay RIGHT on Bay View Trail.

5.2 LEFT at junction with Ridge Fire Road.

5.5 LEFT on Miwok Fire Road for 30 yards, then RIGHT on Oak Ridge Trail.

5.8 Cross fire road to stay on Oak Ridge.

6.2 Cross fire road to stay on Oak Ridge.

6.8 STRAIGHT on Peacock Gap Trail.

6.9 STRAIGHT on Shoreline Trail.

8.7 STRAIGHT on fire road, then RIGHT at restrooms by picnic area to get back on Shoreline Trail.

9.6 LEFT at V-junction.

9.9 LEFT on Shoreline Trail.

10.1 LEFT on Shoreline Trail.

11.6 Arrive at starting point.

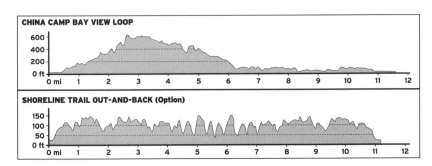

14 THREE LAKES LOOP
Marin Municipal Water District near Ross

DIRT ROAD

Difficulty: 2

Riding Time: 1.5 hours

Total Distance: 11.2 miles

Elevation Gain: 900 feet

Summary: This lake-filled ride in the Marin Watershed is bound to get beginning and intermediate mountain bikers hooked on the sport.

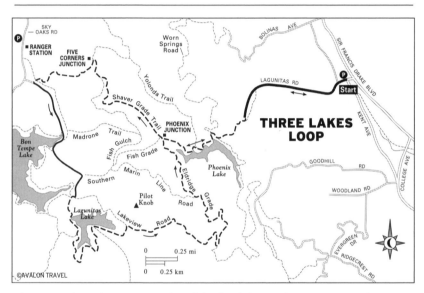

Phoenix Lake is the most popular of the five lakes in the Mount Tamalpais Watershed, but due to a cruel twist of fate it also has the smallest parking lot, with space for only about 15 cars. That means that the hundreds of anglers, hikers, equestrians, baby stroller–pushers, and mountain bikers who want access to Phoenix Lake on summer weekends have to fight it out for a parking space. No street parking is available anywhere near the lake on weekends and holidays (the well-to-do residents of Ross have made sure that their streets are clearly signed and the No Parking rule is strictly enforced), so it's a good thing you're on two wheels. Unless it's a weekday, you must ride a short stretch on the street to gain access to this terrific lake-filled loop.

It's best to leave your car at the large parking lot at Ross Commons Park and pedal from there. A 1.1-mile ride brings you to the jam-packed parking lot at Natalie Coffin Greene Park. Go around the gate and uphill to Phoenix Lake's dam. You've arrived at the first lake of the Three Lakes Loop. Ride around the

Lagunitas Lake is the oldest and loveliest of the watershed reservoirs on the Three Lakes Loop.

right side of the lake, passing a log cabin built in 1893, then climb uphill on Shaver Grade through dense redwoods to join the paved access road to Bon Tempe and Lagunitas Lakes. After briefly skirting the edge of Bon Tempe Lake, you'll face the best scenery of the day as you circle Lagunitas Lake, crossing three small bridges. Make sure you utilize the bridges and don't take shortcuts across the streams. These waterways are important habitat for newts and other amphibians. Lagunitas is the oldest of the Marin lakes; its dam was built in 1873. Both Lagunitas and Bon Tempe Lakes are great spots for bird-watching and fishing.

Too soon, you leave the water behind and face a climb up Lakeview Fire Road. Don't forget to turn around and check out the trail's promised "lake view." The final stretch of the loop follows Eldridge Grade, one of the first wagon routes to the summit of Mount Tamalpais, built in 1889. Be cautious on the steep descent on this old, well-worn trail, which has been reduced to single-track in some stretches.

For more information on Marin Municipal Water District lands, phone Sky Oaks Ranger Station at 415/945-1181 or visit www.marinwater.org.

Driving Directions

From San Francisco, cross the Golden Gate Bridge and drive north on U.S. 101 for 7.5 miles. Take the Sir Francis Drake Boulevard exit west toward San Anselmo, then drive 3 miles to Lagunitas Road on the left, across from the Marin Art and Garden Center. Turn left on Lagunitas Road and park at Ross Commons (junction of Lagunitas and Kent Roads).

Route Directions

0.0 Park at Ross Commons. Ride west on Lagunitas Road. *Supplies are available in Ross.*

1.1 Natalie Coffin Greene Park parking lot; go around the gate and across the bridge, climbing up to Phoenix Lake's dam.

1.4 RIGHT to head around the lake.

1.6 LEFT at junction with Worn Springs Road on the right. *Water is available.*

2.0 RIGHT on Shaver Grade at four-way Phoenix Junction.

3.2 LEFT to stay on Shaver Grade at Five Corners Junction.

3.8 LEFT at gate on paved Sky Oaks Road.

4.3 Ride along edge of Bon Tempe Lake on paved road.

5.1 Lake Lagunitas parking lot. Stay on right side of parking lot to pick up the dirt road leading up to the right side of the dam.

5.7 LEFT at junction with Rock Springs/Lagunitas Fire Road; stay along the lakeshore.

6.5 RIGHT on Lakeview Fire Road.

7.1 LEFT on Eldridge Grade.

8.4 RIGHT to stay on Eldridge Grade (trail narrows considerably).

9.2 RIGHT at Phoenix Junction; backtrack alongside Phoenix Lake and back to Lagunitas Road.

11.2 Arrive at starting point.

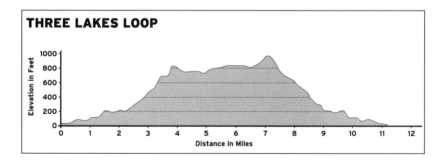

THREE LAKES LOOP

15 STINSON BEACH AND MOUNT TAMALPAIS LOOP
Mount Tamalpais State Park

BEST ☾

PAVED ROADS WITH MODERATE CAR TRAFFIC

Difficulty: 4   **Total Distance:** 23.9 miles

Riding Time: 3 hours   **Elevation Gain:** 2,700 feet

Summary: A day on less-traveled roads showcases the wonders of Mount Tamalpais, from coast to mountaintop.

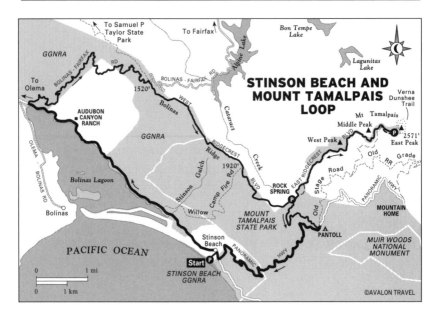

This ride is a workout, but it's well worth it, considering the film-burning quality of the Marin landscape you'll traverse. A level, four-mile warm-up alongside Bolinas Lagoon on Highway 1 is followed by a circuitous and unrelenting 1,500-foot climb up the historic Bolinas–Fairfax stage road. When at last you reach the top, prepare yourself for one of the Bay Area's most filmed and photographed roads—West Ridgecrest Boulevard on Mount Tamalpais, site of dozens of car commercials and calendar shots. The trees give way to open grassy hillsides, where deer graze and hang gliders take off for a breezy, graceful descent to the ocean below. You'll keep climbing as you travel the ridge, but much more gradually from here onward.

At Rock Springs parking lot and road junction, continue straight for another 2.9 miles to Mount Tamalpais's East Peak at elevation 2,571 feet. The vistas are even

© ANN MARIE BROWN

As you get closer to the summit of 2,571-foot Mount Tamalpais, take a break and enjoy the panoramic view of Marin County.

better from this summit than what you've seen so far. In addition to the bird's-eye view out to sea, much of Marin County and San Francisco comes into full perspective. East Peak's snack stand is open on weekends to refuel hungry bikers. When you've had your fill of snacks and views, backtrack to the Rock Springs parking lot.

Now it's time for a steep, fast, memorable descent. The traffic will pick up as you drop to Pantoll Ranger Station, and it will continue racing downhill to the ocean, but you'll be rolling along just as fast, or maybe faster, than the cars. Since you are riding on aptly named Panoramic Highway, take a break now and then to admire the views of the coast ahead and Mount Tamalpais behind.

With a final screech of brakes, you come to a stop sign at Highway 1. A right turn and you're back at your car in less than 0.5 mile. Hope you brought your swimsuit for a dip in the ocean at Stinson Beach, or your wallet for a well-deserved meal at the beachside hamburger stand.

For more information, contact Mount Tamalpais State Park, 415/388-2070, www.parks.ca.gov.

Driving Directions

From San Francisco, cross the Golden Gate Bridge and drive north on U.S. 101 for 4 miles. Take the Mill Valley/Stinson Beach/Highway 1 exit and continue straight for 1 mile to a stoplight at Shoreline Highway (Highway 1). Turn left on Shoreline Highway and drive 12 miles to Stinson Beach. Turn left at the sign for Stinson Beach parking (Golden Gate National Recreation Area).

Route Directions

0.0 Park at Stinson Beach parking lot, ride out to Highway 1, and turn left (north). *Supplies are available in the town of Stinson Beach.*

1.0 Edge of Bolinas Lagoon; look for hauled-out seals and a wide variety of birds.

3.3 Audubon Canyon Ranch. *The ranch, a major great egret nesting site, is open to the public on weekends and holidays mid-March–mid-July. Walk a 0.5-mile trail to a viewing platform, then look through sighting scopes into the nests of baby egrets.*

4.3 RIGHT on Bolinas–Fairfax Road (unsigned paved road with open metal gate). Begin 4.4-mile climb.

8.7 RIGHT on West Ridgecrest Boulevard.

12.5 STRAIGHT at Rock Springs parking lot.

15.4 East Peak parking lot; TURN AROUND. *Water and snacks are available. Lock your bike and walk the one-mile Verna Dunshee Trail that circumnavigates the peak.*

18.3 LEFT at Rock Springs parking lot.

19.8 RIGHT on Panoramic Highway at Pantoll junction. *Water is available across the road by the ranger station.*

23.5 RIGHT on Highway 1.

23.9 LEFT into Stinson Beach parking lot; arrive at starting point.

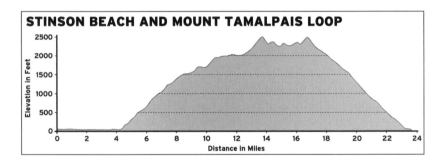

STINSON BEACH AND MOUNT TAMALPAIS LOOP

16 OLD STAGE ROAD AND OLD RAILROAD GRADE TO EAST PEAK   BEST ☾

Mount Tamalpais State Park

DIRT ROAD

Difficulty: 2

Riding Time: 1.5 hours

Total Distance: 8 miles

Elevation Gain: 1,100 feet

Summary: Take a ride through Mount Tamalpais history on this out-and-back trip to its 2,571-foot East Peak.

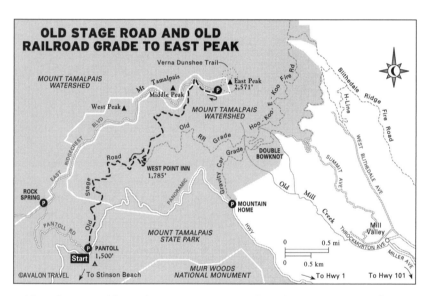

Although you could just drive your car on paved roads to Mount Tam's famous summit, this ride on a stretch of the old Mount Tamalpais Scenic Railway is a much more enjoyable way to get there.

The railway, known in the early 1900s as the "Crookedest Railroad in the World," carried passengers through 281 turns and curves up the slopes of Mount Tamalpais. The last two miles of this ride trace the train's exact route to the mountain summit, while the first two miles follow the route used by passengers who rode the stagecoach to Stinson Beach and Bolinas. (See ride 17, *Old Railroad Grade to West Point Inn,* for more riding on Old Railroad Grade.) The two halves of this ride converge at West Point Inn, as much a popular stopover for cyclists and hikers today as it was for train and stage passengers 100 years ago.

Begin your ride at the large parking area by Pantoll Ranger Station. After a

The historic Old Stage Road provides views of Angel Island, southern Marin County, and the San Francisco skyline.

hasty and cautious crossing of Panoramic Highway, mount your bike and follow the paved Old Stage Road. The pavement soon turns to dirt, and the views of San Francisco and Marin start to amaze you. Old Stage Road's grade is remarkably gradual as it winds through myriad twists and turns.

At West Point Inn, fill up your water bottle at their old stone fountain, or buy a glass of lemonade and have a seat on the outside deck, then pick up Old Railroad Grade on the inn's west side and continue uphill to East Peak. This dirt road is steeper, and much rockier, than Old Stage Road. At the trail's end you'll find yourself at the paved East Peak parking lot, enjoying far-reaching views of Marin County, the East Bay, and San Francisco and its bridges. Be sure to walk up the stairs to the Gardner Fire Lookout so you can say you went to the tip-top of the mountain.

For more information, contact Mount Tamalpais State Park, 415/388-2070, www.parks.ca.gov. Contact the West Point Inn at 415/388-9955 or 415/646-0702, www.westpointinn.com (closed on Monday; summer hours 11 A.M.–6 P.M., winter hours 11 A.M.–5 P.M.).

Options

If you don't want to ride back the way you came, you can always follow the paved route back to Pantoll: Take West Ridgecrest Boulevard 2.9 miles to Rock Springs, then turn left on Pantoll Road and ride 1.5 miles downhill, for an 8.4-mile loop. This is a fun loop if you don't mind competing with car traffic.

Driving Directions

From San Francisco, cross the Golden Gate Bridge and drive north on U.S. 101 for 4 miles. Take the Mill Valley/Stinson Beach/Highway 1 exit and continue straight for 1 mile to a stoplight at Shoreline Highway (Highway 1). Turn left on Shoreline Highway and drive 2.5 miles, then turn right on Panoramic Highway. Drive 0.9 mile to a junction of roads. Continue straight 4.3 miles farther to Pantoll Ranger Station and the parking lot on the left.

Route Directions

0.0 Park by Pantoll Ranger Station, then cross Panoramic Highway to the start of Pantoll Road. On the right is a paved road signed Old Stage Road to East Peak. *Supplies are available in Mill Valley.*

0.1 Begin riding on Old Stage Road.

0.4 Pavement turns to dirt.

2.0 West Point Inn. After enjoying the view, pick up Old Railroad Grade on the left (west) side of the inn. *Water and snacks are available.*

4.0 RIGHT on pavement at East Peak parking lot; TURN AROUND. *A small visitor center, overlook area, and the Gardner Fire Lookout are located here. Walk the Verna Dunshee Trail or climb the stairs to the lookout for the best view of the day.*

8.0 Arrive at starting point.

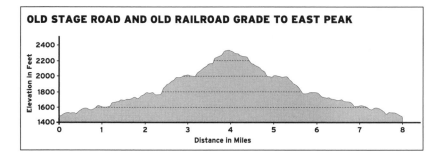

OLD STAGE ROAD AND OLD RAILROAD GRADE TO EAST PEAK

17 OLD RAILROAD GRADE TO WEST POINT INN

Mill Valley to Mount Tamalpais

DIRT ROAD

Difficulty: 3 | **Total Distance:** 13.8 miles (or 17.8-mile option)

Riding Time: 2 hours | **Elevation Gain:** 1,700 feet

Summary: One of Marin County's most popular mountain bike routes follows the trail of a historic railroad up the slopes of Mount Tamalpais.

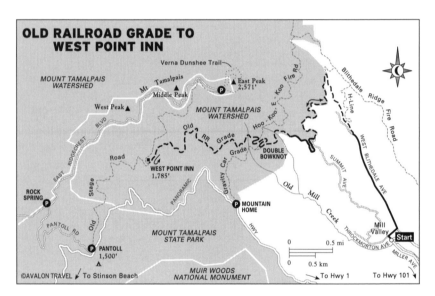

Beginning in Mill Valley, this popular ride on the slopes of Mount Tamalpais follows the lower route of the "Crookedest Railroad in the World," a major tourist attraction that carried passengers up the mountain in the early 1900s. Your destination is historic West Point Inn, built in 1904 to serve railway passengers and still serving cyclists and hikers today. The inn has small cabins for rent and sells drinks and snacks. Its water fountain will come in handy after you ride these 6.9 ascending (and dusty in summer) miles.

Downtown Mill Valley is Cyclist Central on fair-weather weekends. You'll have to park a mile or so from the start of Old Railroad Grade; there is almost no parking at the trailhead. From downtown, follow West Blithedale Road to the Marin Open Space District gate at the start of the railroad grade. This is your level warm-up; soon you start to climb on a remarkably consistent grade. The lower

© ANN MARIE BROWN

Mountain bikers use historic West Point Inn as a rest stop on the ascent up Mount Tamalpais.

portion of the trail is heavily shaded by redwoods and Douglas firs; you won't start to feel the summer heat until you ascend above the tree canopy. A highlight of the ride is the double bowknot, where the railroad curved through a series of tight, gradual switchbacks. You'll know it when you ride it.

This trail is an excellent choice for mountain bikers who have progressed past the beginner stage but aren't interested (or ready for) very technical riding. It offers a solid aerobic and leg workout with only minor challenges from rocks and ruts. And the big carrot is that West Point Inn provides a scenic and relaxing destination.

For more information, contact Mount Tamalpais State Park, 415/388-2070, www.parks.ca.gov; or Marin Municipal Water District, 415/945-1195. The West Point Inn can be reached at 415/388-9955 or 415/646-0702, www.westpointinn.com (closed on Monday; summer hours 11 A.M.–6 P.M., winter hours 11 A.M.–5 P.M.).

Options

If you wish to add a few more miles, Old Railroad Grade continues another two miles from West Point Inn to East Peak (see ride 16, *Old Stage Road and Old Railroad Grade to East Peak*). From there, you could retrace your tire treads or loop back on Eldridge Grade, Indian Fire Road, and Hoo Koo E Koo Road. Check the Mount Tamalpais State Park map, available at Pantoll Ranger Station, for details.

Driving Directions

From San Francisco, cross the Golden Gate Bridge and drive north on U.S. 101 for six miles. Take the Tiburon/Highway 131/East Blithedale Avenue exit, then turn left and drive two miles west on East Blithedale. Turn left on Throckmorton Avenue and drive one block to Miller Avenue in downtown Mill Valley.

Route Directions

0.0 Park near the junction of Miller and Throckmorton Avenues in Mill Valley. Ride north on Throckmorton for one block to its junction with East and West Blithedale Avenues. *Supplies are available in the surrounding blocks.*

0.1 LEFT on West Blithedale.

1.4 RIGHT at gate on dirt Old Railroad Grade.

2.1 LEFT at junction.

3.3 RIGHT on pavement (uphill) where dirt road ends.

3.7 Back on dirt road.

4.4 RIGHT at junction; start of double bowknot.

6.9 West Point Inn. TURN AROUND or continue two miles to East Peak. *Water and snacks are usually available.*

13.8 Arrive at starting point.

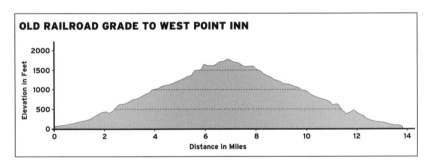

18 TIBURON AND BELVEDERE LOOP BEST 【

Tiburon Peninsula

BIKE PATH AND PAVED ROADS WITH MODERATE CAR TRAFFIC

Difficulty: 2   **Total Distance:** 10.5 miles (or longer options)

Riding Time: 1 hour   **Elevation Gain:** 700 feet

Summary: For easy riding with stunning bay views, you can't do much better than the Tiburon and Belvedere Loop.

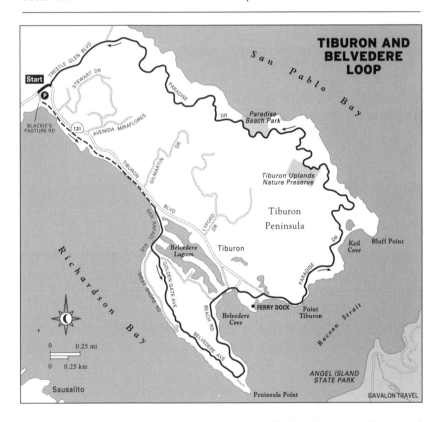

This combined bike path and paved road ride provides the chance to pedal around some prime real estate along scenic San Francisco Bay—the type of property that 99.9 percent of us would never be able to afford in our wildest dreams.

The first part of the ride follows the Tiburon Bike Path from Blackie's Pasture, just outside of the town of Tiburon. The popular trailhead is well known for its large statue of a horse, which was built to commemorate Blackie, who grazed in this pasture until his salad days ended at the ripe old age of 33, in

1966. Local admirers put up a gravestone, and later this handsome statue, in his memory.

The bike path travels east for 2.3 miles into downtown Tiburon, although the ride described here leaves the path after the first mile. This converted rail trail was once the track of the Northwestern Pacific Railroad, which provided passenger and freight service from Corte Madera to Tiburon. The trail provides close-up bay views—the water laps within 20 feet of the trail at high tide—and glimpses of Sausalito, the Golden Gate Bridge, and Mount Tamalpais. At low tide, bird-watching is rewarding, as long-legged shorebirds are perpetually digging in the mudflats for a meal. The trail also passes the Richardson Bay Wildlife Ponds. Managed by the Richardson Bay Sanitary District, these small bird ponds make good use of Tiburon's sewage.

After a right turn on San Rafael Avenue, you'll ride through ultra-wealthy Belvedere neighborhoods and enjoy a free show of multimillion-dollar bay views. The streets narrow to one lane wide; it's a wonder there aren't more collisions between Bentleys and Rolls Royces. Stay as far to the right as you can. Next you'll drop into downtown Tiburon, which is usually packed with tourists on weekends. Hang out with the crowds and explore the shops, or make a quick escape by turning right on Paradise Drive and climbing your first serious hill, which lasts for nearly a half mile. You'll stay on well-named Paradise Drive for most of the rest of this ride. Although the road is extremely narrow and has virtually no shoulder, traffic is generally light and cars must drive slowly because of its multiple winding curves. As you wind northward, the houses eventually become fewer and farther between, and views of north San Pablo Bay open wide. You'll pass the entrance to Paradise Beach Park, a popular hangout on summer weekends. People come from all over Marin County for swimming and sunning here. Too soon, you reach a junction with Trestle Glen Drive and must turn back to Blackie's Pasture.

Options

Multiple options for extending this ride are possible. Many cyclists start in Mill Valley or Sausalito and ride to Blackie's instead of driving there (most of the route can be traveled on bike paths). Some riders begin their trip in San Francisco, follow the Sausalito and Mill Valley bike paths to Tiburon, cruise around this loop, have lunch at a local restaurant, then take the easy way home—by riding the ferry back to San Francisco. Those who are more ambitious simply ride back. No matter how you do it, it's a fine way to spend a day.

Driving Directions

From San Francisco, cross the Golden Gate Bridge and drive north on U.S. 101

for 6 miles. Take the Tiburon/Highway 131/East Blithedale Avenue exit and drive east for 1.5 miles, then turn right at Blackie's Pasture Road and park in the large parking lot.

Route Directions

0.0 Park at Blackie's Pasture parking lot. Ride east on the paved bike trail. *Supplies are available in Mill Valley or Tiburon.*

1.2 RIGHT on San Rafael Avenue (leave bike path).

1.6 LEFT to stay on San Rafael Avenue.

1.7 RIGHT on Golden Gate Avenue and up the hill.

1.9 STRAIGHT at stop sign.

2.0 Cross intersection and continue on Belvedere Avenue (straight and slightly to the right).

3.2 RIGHT on Beach Road.

3.5 RIGHT to stay on Beach Road.

3.8 STRAIGHT at stop sign (stay on Beach Road).

4.0 RIGHT on Main Street. *Supplies are available in downtown Tiburon.*

4.3 RIGHT on Paradise Drive.

6.6 Trailhead for Tiburon Uplands Nature Preserve on left (hiking trail only).

7.6 Paradise Beach Park on right. *Water is available.*

9.7 LEFT on Trestle Glen Drive.

10.2 Cross Tiburon Boulevard at stoplight and crosswalk; pick up bike path on far side and ride west (to your right).

10.4 LEFT into Blackie's Pasture parking lot.

10.5 Arrive at starting point.

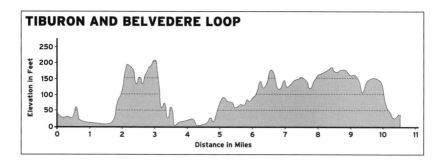

TIBURON AND BELVEDERE LOOP

19 TENNESSEE VALLEY AND COYOTE RIDGE LOOP

Golden Gate National Recreation Area near Mill Valley

DIRT ROAD AND SINGLE-TRACK

Difficulty: 3   **Total Distance:** 6.5 miles

Riding Time: 1.5 hours   **Elevation Gain:** 1,200 feet

Summary: While training wheels and Burley trailers ride an easy out-and-back to Tennessee Beach, those seeking more of a workout explore the high ridges above.

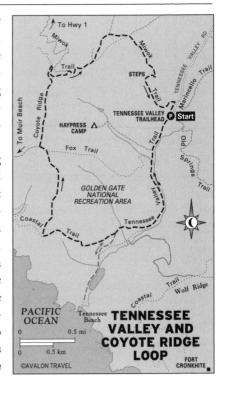

On weekends, the Tennessee Valley Trailhead in Mill Valley is busier than a shopping mall at Christmas. The parking lot is filled with a mix of bikers, walkers, and runners, all wanting to get a piece of the scenery at Tennessee Valley Beach and/or its surrounding ridges and hillsides.

And no wonder: There's something for everyone here. Biking families and novice riders enjoy the easy, wide dirt road that rolls gently out to Tennessee Beach, a black-gravel pocket beach framed by jagged bluffs on both sides. Mountain bikers seeking more of a challenge choose from two possible loops: Tennessee Valley and Coyote Ridge to the west or Miwok and Bobcat to the east. (The latter loop can also be accessed from the Marin Headlands and is described in ride 20, *Marin Headlands Miwok and Bobcat Loop.*)

Those simply following Tennessee Valley Trail to the beach will find the path amazingly easy and scenic. Bring a bike lock (a bike rack is provided) and a picnic for the picturesque beach, and be sure to hike up the short trail on the north bluff for a memorable view of the coast.

The longer loop described here takes off 0.6 mile before the beach (might as well ride over and check it out first, since you're here), then makes a short but

Lock up your bike, take off your cycling shoes, and explore the black sands of Tennessee Beach.

hellacious climb up Coastal Trail. At the summit, catch your breath and enjoy the views, because there's more climbing ahead on Coyote Ridge Trail. A final downhill stint on Miwok Trail will bring you back to Tennessee Valley Trailhead with some exciting—and surprisingly technical—single-track. (Don't let the railroad-tie stairs 0.5 mile from the end catch you by surprise.) This loop's total mileage is short, but the steep uphills and rutted dirt trails dole out a solid workout. And it goes without saying that the Marin Headlands scenery never disappoints.

For more information, contact Golden Gate National Recreation Area, 415/331-1540, www.nps.gov/goga.

Driving Directions

From San Francisco, cross the Golden Gate Bridge and drive north on U.S. 101 for 4 miles. Take the Mill Valley/Stinson Beach/Highway 1 exit and continue straight for 0.6 mile to Tennessee Valley Road on the left. Turn left and drive 2 miles to the trailhead.

Route Directions

0.0 Park at Tennessee Valley Trailhead and follow the main, wide road southwest. *Supplies are available in Mill Valley, two miles north.*

1.3 STRAIGHT at junction with Coastal Trail.

1.9 Tennessee Beach bike rack. TURN AROUND.

2.5 LEFT at junction with Coastal Trail; hill climb.

3.1 RIGHT at junction.

3.8 LEFT then immediate RIGHT on Coyote Ridge Trail.

4.3 STRAIGHT at two Green Gulch junctions.

4.4 High point and end of climb.

4.6 STRAIGHT on Miwok Trail.

5.4 RIGHT to stay on Miwok Trail.

5.6 STRAIGHT on Miwok at junction with Countryview Road Trail on left.

6.5 Arrive at starting point.

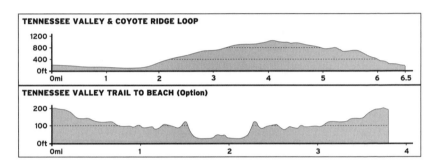

20 MARIN HEADLANDS MIWOK AND BOBCAT LOOP

Golden Gate National Recreation Area near Sausalito

DIRT ROAD AND SINGLE-TRACK; PAVED ROADS WITH MODERATE CAR TRAFFIC

Difficulty: 4   **Total Distance:** 14 miles

Riding Time: 2 hours   **Elevation Gain:** 2,100 feet

Summary: Just across from the Golden Gate Bridge, this scenic ride takes you far from city life into the wonders of the Marin Headlands.

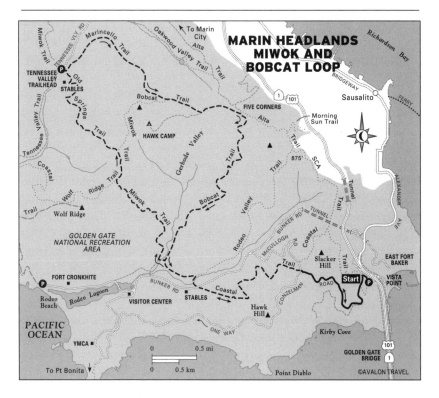

Riders can choose from many possible starting points for this loop: the San Francisco or Marin sides of the Golden Gate Bridge, the Tennessee Valley Trailhead in Mill Valley, the Rodeo Avenue exit off U.S. 101 near Sausalito, or Rodeo Beach at the Marin Headlands. The ride described here starts from the Conzelman parking lot on the northwest side of the Golden Gate Bridge because that allows for the most off-road miles. (Three of the total 14 miles

The long climb on the Miwok Trail to the top of Wolf Ridge in the Marin Headlands will get your heart and lungs pumping.

are paved; the rest are wide fire roads and single-track.) Ride this loop any way you like; it's all good.

Like the other Marin Headlands loop described in this book (see ride 19, *Tennessee Valley and Coyote Ridge Loop*), this route offers ocean views, grasslands, wildflowers, and coastal hills. Two significant climbs will get your heart and lungs pumping. One is a 1.5-mile stretch on Miwok Trail from Rodeo Valley up to the top of Wolf Ridge. The other is the 1.5-mile Marincello Trail heading uphill from Tennessee Valley. At least the ascents are memorable: You'll gain some wide blue-water views. One other potential problem is the encroaching poison oak on Coastal Trail. Sometimes the Park Service maintains this trail; sometimes not. Better carry some Tecnu (a lotion used to treat poison oak) just in case.

A highlight is Bobcat Trail, which drops through one of the Bay Area's most special places, the Gerbode Valley. This beautiful valley was just barely saved from development in the 1960s, when a community for 20,000 people was planned for the area. With your first glimpse of Gerbode Valley, you'll grimace at the thought of developers paving over its pristine grasslands. Chalk up a victory for the hawks, butterflies, and bobcats. And yes, the latter are often seen on Bobcat Trail.

For more information, contact Golden Gate National Recreation Area, 415/331-1540, www.nps.gov/goga.

Options

A backpacking camp is found 0.5 mile off Bobcat Trail, so you could turn this ride into an overnight adventure. Don't overload your mountain bike's panniers, however, or these hills will be very unforgiving.

Driving Directions

From San Francisco, cross the Golden Gate Bridge on U.S. 101 and take the first exit north of the bridge, Alexander Avenue. Turn left and loop back under the freeway, then turn right on Conzelman Road (signed for Marin Headlands). Park in the lot on the left, 100 feet up the road.

Route Directions

0.0 Park at lot at start of Conzelman Road, on the northwest side of the Golden Gate Bridge. Ride out of the parking lot and turn left and uphill on Conzelman. *Supplies are available in Sausalito, two miles away.*

1.3 RIGHT at junction with McCullough Road (paved); then LEFT on signed, dirt Coastal Trail (beware of poison oak).

2.9 STRAIGHT at junction to cross paved Bunker Road.

3.0 LEFT on Rodeo Valley Trail.

3.4 LEFT on Bobcat Trail at Y-junction.

3.5 RIGHT on Miwok Trail; now you're on the loop; steep climb ahead.

4.6 RIGHT to stay on Miwok at junction with Wolf Ridge Trail.

4.9 LEFT on Old Springs Trail (single-track; can be very rutted).

6.2 Stables at Tennessee Valley Trailhead. Walk your bike through stables and parking lot and pick up Marincello Trail on right (northeast) edge of lot; prepare to climb.

7.7 LEFT on Bobcat Trail.

8.5 RIGHT to stay on Bobcat at junction with Rodeo and Alta Trails; steep descent into Gerbode Valley begins.

10.5 LEFT on Rodeo Valley Trail at end of loop; backtrack on Rodeo Valley Trail, Coastal Trail, and Conzelman Road to parking lot.

14.0 Arrive at starting point.

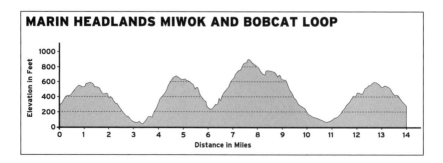

MARIN HEADLANDS MIWOK AND BOBCAT LOOP

21 PERIMETER TRAIL AND FIRE ROAD LOOPS

Angel Island State Park

BEST ☾

DIRT ROAD AND DETERIORATING PAVEMENT

Difficulty: 2

Total Distance: 9.6 miles

Riding Time: 2 hours

Elevation Gain: 900 feet

Summary: The most desirable real estate in the Bay Area is yours for the day on this view-filled ride on Angel Island.

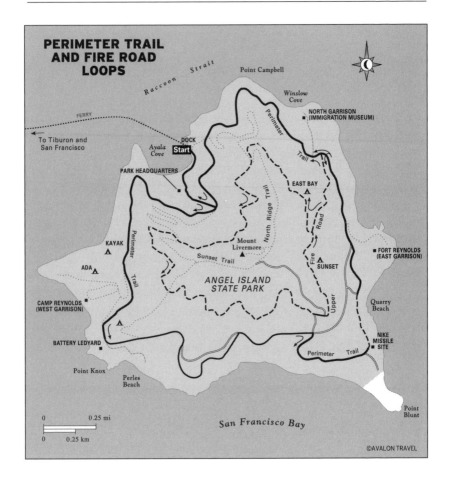

© ANN MARIE BROWN

view of the Bay Bridge and San Francisco from Angel Island's Perimeter Trail

The Perimeter Trail at Angel Island State Park provides 360-degree views from its setting in the middle of the bay, making it arguably the most scenic bike trail in the entire Bay Area. Views change constantly as you pedal, allowing you to see the cities and towns surrounding the bay in an entirely new perspective. One of the best vistas lies on the southeast side of the island, where an open stretch captures the Bay and Golden Gate Bridges, plus Alcatraz Island. The 180-degree scene encompasses the whole sweep of urban skylines from Berkeley to San Francisco to Sausalito.

And the island doles out more than just views. Bikers can also enjoy two sandy beaches just off the trail, a wealth of historic sites, and the simple joy of a boat trip—a half-hour ferry cruise from various cities around the bay.

Perimeter Trail is a partially paved road, with the pavement deteriorating to gravel and dirt in places. True to its name, the trail loops around the island's perimeter, so you can ride your bike in either direction (the route suggested here goes counterclockwise). History lessons are readily available because Angel Island has had a long and varied past as a military outpost, a Russian sea otter hunters' site, and an immigrant detention center. Be sure to read the interpretive signs around the island or stop in at the visitor center near Ayala Cove to get more information.

Many island visitors are satisfied to ride only the 5.5-mile Perimeter Trail, but if you'd like to get away from the crowds and enjoy some more exercise, you can connect to a loop-within-the-loop, a dirt fire road on the island's interior. The route suggested here connects the two loops at the fire station on the north side of the island, but you can also connect them via the cutoff for Mount Livermore on the southeast side. Because the upper fire road is higher in elevation, it offers even more expansive views than Perimeter Trail.

One note of caution: The wind can blow at Angel Island, and the fog can come in on a moment's notice, so come prepared with an extra jacket, even on sunny days.

For more information, contact Angel Island State Park, 415/435-1915, www.angelisland.org.

Driving Directions

Ferry service to Angel Island is available from Tiburon, San Francisco, and Oakland/Alameda. For Tiburon departures, contact the Tiburon Ferry at 415/435-2131, www.angelislandferry.com. For Oakland or Alameda departures, contact East Bay Ferry at 510/522-3300, www.eastbayferry.com. For San Francisco departures, contact Blue and Gold Fleet at 415/773-1188, www.blueandgoldfleet.com.

Route Directions

0.0 Arrive at ferry landing at Ayala Cove. Retrieve your bike from the ferry and ride to your right, past the café and toward the picnic area. *Water, pay phones, restrooms, and rental lockers are available at the ferry landing; food is available at the landing café.*

0.2 LEFT on gravel bike trail by picnic area.

0.5 RIGHT on Perimeter Trail.

1.3 West Garrison and Camp Reynolds.

1.7 Cutoff for road to Perle's Beach; views of San Francisco and Alcatraz from the beach.

2.9 STRAIGHT on Perimeter Trail at junction with upper Fire Road.

3.5 East Garrison and old military hospital.

3.9 LEFT at junction with upper Fire Road at Fire Station.

4.3 RIGHT on Fire Road.

7.7 RIGHT on connecting road back to Perimeter Trail.

8.0 LEFT on Perimeter Trail.

9.1 RIGHT at junction with trail to Ayala Cove.

9.6 Arrive at starting point.

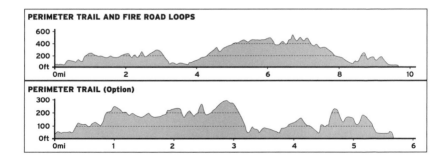

22 GOLDEN GATE BRIDGE AND MARIN HEADLANDS LOOP BEST (

Golden Gate National Recreation Area near Sausalito

PAVED ROADS WITH MODERATE CAR TRAFFIC

Difficulty: 3

Total Distance: 15 miles

Riding Time: 1.5-2 hours

Elevation Gain: 1,500 feet

Summary: A favorite training ride for city cyclists, this loop is also ideal for visitors seeking a true taste of the City by the Bay and its environs.

This ride is classic San Francisco, with vista after vista of world-class scenery. Beginning at Fort Point in San Francisco's Presidio, the route crosses the Golden Gate Bridge, then follows Conzelman Road through the Marin Headlands, with frequent jaw-dropping views back toward the mouth of the Golden Gate. A challenging climb up to Hawk Hill (920 feet) is followed by a dizzying descent on cliffside Conzelman Road, which thankfully is one-way in this stretch. Make sure your brakes are working well before you begin the precipitous drop.

At the edge of the headlands, a narrow strip of land curves out to Point Bonita Lighthouse, which can be visited via a one-mile round-trip walk. Time your trip carefully: The 1855-built lighthouse is open only on Saturday, Sunday, and

© ANN MARIE BROWN

Rodeo Beach is an excellent spot to take a break on the Golden Gate Bridge and Marin Headlands Loop.

GOLDEN GATE BRIDGE AND
MARIN HEADLANDS LOOP

©AVALON TRAVEL

Monday 12:30–3:30 P.M., and is accessed via a 50-foot-long tunnel and 40-yard-long suspension footbridge. Its location is the most dramatic of any lighthouse on the California coast; don't miss seeing it.

Other highlights along the loop include Black Sand Beach, the Marin Headlands Visitor Center, and beautiful Rodeo Beach and Rodeo Lagoon. With all these places to visit, a bike lock is more than a good idea. The trip back includes a ride through a long, lighted tunnel with bike lanes, and then another jaunt across the magnificent Golden Gate Bridge.

Use some caution in crossing the bridge, especially if you ride on a weekday, when you must use the east sidewalk (shared with oblivious pedestrians toting video cameras). On weekends, cyclists ride on the west sidewalk while pedestrians use the east sidewalk, so there's less congestion. Either way, keep your speed down and take time to enjoy the view from 225 feet above San Francisco Bay.

For more information, contact Golden Gate National Recreation Area, 415/331-1540, www.nps.gov/goga.

Driving Directions

From the Crissy Field and marina area of San Francisco, take Lincoln Boulevard west toward the Golden Gate Bridge. Turn right just before the bridge entrance into the Battery East parking lot at Fort Point.

Route Directions

0.0 Park at the Battery East parking lot at Fort Point on Lincoln Boulevard (east side of the Golden Gate Bridge). At the entrance to the parking lot is a gated, paved road that is signed as a bike route (#202) to get on the bridge. *Water and snacks are available at Bridge Cafe at the bridge entrance (Bridge View Area).*

0.2 Start across the Golden Gate Bridge (ride on west side on weekends and holidays and east side on weekdays; obey all posted instruction signs for cyclists).

1.8 LEFT up hill on Conzelman Road at north (Marin County) side of Golden Gate Bridge. *If you're on the east sidewalk, exit at the Vista Point area and take the stairway underpass under the highway to the start of Conzelman Road. If you're on the west sidewalk, follow the signs for cyclists to the start of Conzelman Road.*

3.5 LEFT at junction with McCullough Road.

4.1 Summit of Hawk Hill; two-way road turns to one-way and descent begins.

5.0 Parking lot for Black Sand Beach on left. *Lock up your bike and hike 0.5 mile to one of Marin County's most spectacular beaches.*

6.0 STRAIGHT for Point Bonita Lighthouse.

6.5 Lighthouse trailhead. *Lock up your bike and hike 0.5 mile to the lighthouse.*

6.7 Road ends at Battery Mendell and overlook. TURN AROUND.

7.8 Marin Headlands Visitor Center on left.

8.0 LEFT at junction with Bunker Road.

8.5 LEFT at junction; Marin Mammal Center above to the right.

8.9 Road ends at Rodeo Beach parking lot. TURN AROUND. *Lock up your bike and explore the beach and lagoon trail. Mountain bikers can continue up Coastal Trail (gated road) 1.6 miles from parking lot to the top of Hill 88 and a spectacular view; a turnaround is required at the top.*

10.0 LEFT at junction of Field Road and Bunker Road.

12.2 Entrance to one-way tunnel. Push the button to alert motorists that a cyclist is in the tunnel.

12.7 Exit tunnel and ride uphill.

12.9 RIGHT at stop sign.

13.2 Start of Conzelman Road. Return to proper side of the bridge according to day of the week.

15.0 Arrive at starting point.

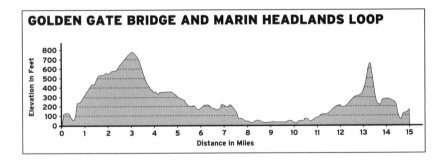

GOLDEN GATE BRIDGE AND MARIN HEADLANDS LOOP

EAST BAY

© ANN MARIE BROWN

BEST BIKE RIDES

⟨ Families
Nimitz Way and Wildcat Canyon, **page 106.**

⟨ High Overlooks
Mount Diablo Summit Ride, **page 137.**

⟨ Wildlife-Viewing
Alameda Creek Trail, **page 157.**

If it's sunny-day riding you seek, your best chance

to find it in the San Francisco Bay Area is in the East Bay. Here, a bit farther from the ocean's influence, is the Bay Area's driest microclimate, where even the infamous summer fog rarely penetrates. The East Bay landscape comprises oak-dotted hills, grassy ridgelines, forested valleys, and rock-studded peaks. Two major East Bay counties – Alameda and Contra Costa – are home to 2.6 million people, many who find escape from the numerous freeways and office complexes by heading to the lands managed by the East Bay Regional Park District (EBRPD). With more than 100,000 acres of land under its jurisdiction, the district operates 65 separate parks and preserves containing a whopping 1,200 miles of trails, approximately half of which are open to bikes.

And those trails are not just for mountain bikers. The East Bay is nationally recognized for its wealth of paved bike paths, most of which had their beginnings as railroad right-of-ways. Several paved recreation trails are managed by the EBRPD, including the Lafayette-Moraga Regional Trail, Iron Horse Regional Trail, and Alameda Creek Trail. Additionally, the roads that border many of the EBRPD's parks and preserves are favored routes of road cyclists. Of particular note is Skyline Boulevard, which travels the spine of the Oakland and Berkeley hills, passing Sibley Volcanic Regional Preserve, Huckleberry Botanic Regional Preserve, Redwood Regional Park, and Anthony Chabot Regional Park. On sunny weekend days, the two-lane road often seems to have more cycling traffic than automobile traffic.

The State of California also has a hand in managing the East Bay's bountiful natural resources. Anchoring the northeast corner of the East Bay is mighty 3,849-foot Mount Diablo, the centerpiece of Mount Diablo State Park. While the park's view-filled summit road is a favorite route of road cyclists, its fire roads are preferred by mountain bikers, except in the hottest months of summer. Due to some strategic land acquisitions in the late 20th century, the state park is now part of a contiguous corridor of East Bay open space that includes Round Valley Regional Preserve, Morgan Territory Regional Preserve, Brushy Peaks Regional Preserve, and the Los Vaqueros Watershed – all of which have trails open to mountain biking.

But if you aren't in the mood for the East Bay's wilder side, there is more "civilized" pedaling to be done in the Livermore Valley, where local wineries open their tasting rooms to Lycra-wearing cyclists. Or, if you're a history buff, the ghost town sites and abandoned shafts at Black Diamond Mines Regional Preserve will attract your curiosity. Bird-watching bicyclists should flock to the shores of San Francisco Bay at Coyote Hills Regional Park, while would-be sailors will prefer the views from their saddles of the shipping lanes at Carquinez Strait. From the salt marshes at the bay's edge to the hot, rocky summit of Mount Diablo, variety is the name of the game for East Bay bicyclists.

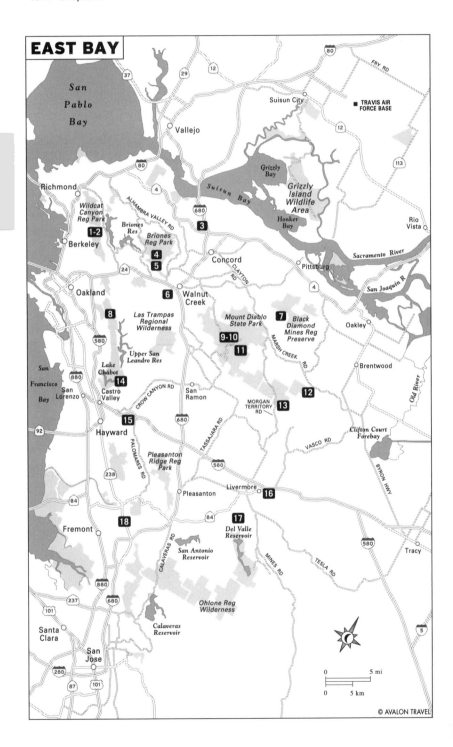

TRAIL NAME	LEVEL	DISTANCE	TIME	ELEVATION	PAGE
1 Nimitz Way and Wildcat Canyon	2	11.3 mi	2 hr	800 ft	106
2 Skyline Loop	3	28.5 mi (or 23-mile option)	2 hr	2,000 ft	109
3 Carquinez Strait Loop	2	18.5 mi	1.5-2 hr	1,200 ft	113
4 Briones Crest Loop	2	8 mi	1.5 hr	1,200 ft	116
5 Three Bears Loop	3	19.5 mi	1.5 hr	1,600 ft	119
6 Lafayette-Moraga Regional Trail	1	15.4 mi	1.5 hr	550 ft	121
7 Stewartville and Ridge Trails Loop	3	10.8 mi	2 hr	1,900 ft	124
8 East and West Ridge Loop	2	9.4 mi	2 hr	1,100 ft	128
9 Wall Point and Barbeque Terrace Loop	3	9.4 mi	2 hr	1,600 ft	131
10 Mitchell and Donner Canyons Loop	4	13.1 mi	2.5 hr	2,900 ft	134
11 Mount Diablo Summit Ride	4	29.6 mi	4-5 hr	3,200 ft	137
12 Round Valley Ramble	1	10.8 mi	1.5 hr	600 ft	140
13 Volvon and Valley View Loop	3	8.4 mi	2 hr	1,200 ft	143
14 Lake Chabot Loop	3	13.3 mi	2 hr	1,200 ft	146
15 Palomares Road	3	20.2 mi	1-2 hr	1,900 ft	149
16 Morgan Territory Road	4	46.4 mi	3-4 hr	3,500 ft	151
17 Livermore Winery Ride	2	19.5 mi	2 hr	800 ft	154
18 Alameda Creek Trail	1	24 mi	2 hr	200 ft	157

1 NIMITZ WAY AND WILDCAT CANYON

BEST [(

Tilden and Wildcat Canyon Regional Parks, Berkeley hills

DIRT ROAD AND PAVED BIKE PATH

Difficulty: 2

Riding Time: 2 hours

Total Distance: 11.3 miles

Elevation Gain: 800 feet

Summary: The East Bay's most scenic paved trail forms one leg of this fun mountain biking loop.

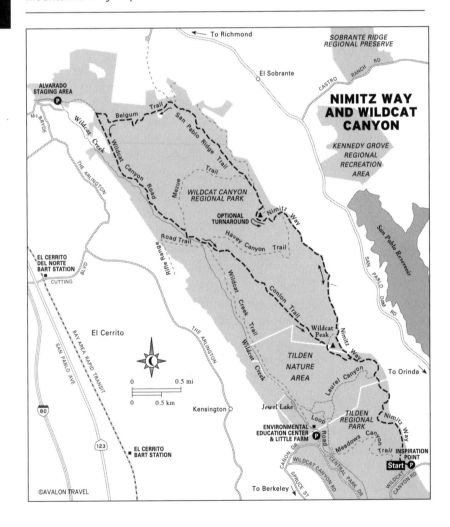

In contrast to the high ridgeline ride on Nimitz Way, Wildcat Creek Trail rolls along the base of Wildcat Canyon, paralleling its stream.

Of all the paved recreation trails in the East Bay, Nimitz Way wins the prize for best views. Perched on the tip of San Pablo Ridge in Tilden Park, the trail serves up nonstop scenery variations. Near its start, cyclists survey San Pablo Reservoir, with Briones Reservoir behind, plus looming Mount Diablo. A few pedal cranks later, San Francisco Bay, the Golden Gate Bridge, and Angel Island come into view. At every turn in the trail, over every hill, you gain a different perspective. First the Richmond Bridge appears, next the Gold Coast shows up, soon San Francisco's skyline emerges, and finally the Brothers Islands steal the scene. On a clear day, the ever-changing panorama will amaze you.

Paved Nimitz Way is mostly level with only one short hill right before the pavement ends at 3.9 miles. It is well loved by every kind of rider, including those on tricycles and training wheels, and with good reason. Mountain bikers use Nimitz Way to connect to dirt trails in Tilden and Wildcat Canyon parks. The ride described here is an easy-to-moderate loop through Wildcat Canyon that affords a good workout, memorable views, and the chance to spot hawks, bunnies, and even a bobcat in the grassy hills of Wildcat Canyon. Be forewarned that the loop has two very steep downhills, where I've seen riders walking their bikes while simultaneously biting their nails. Hey, at least you don't have to ride *up* those hills.

If you're planning on riding in this area on the weekend, get to the Inspiration Point parking lot early. The place is Bike City every Saturday and Sunday, and parking spots are at a premium.

For more information, contact East Bay Regional Park District, 510/562-7275 or 510/635-0135, www.ebparks.org.

Driving Directions

From I-580 in Oakland, take Highway 24 east. Go through the Caldecott Tunnel and exit at Orinda. Turn left on Camino Pablo. Drive north for 2 miles, then turn left on Wildcat Canyon Road. Drive 2.4 miles to the Inspiration Point parking lot.

Route Directions

0.0 Park at Inspiration Point parking lot and take the well-signed Nimitz Way Trail. *Supplies are available in Berkeley or Orinda.*

3.9 End of paved Nimitz Way Trail. Go through gate to join dirt San Pablo Ridge Trail; ignore trails branching right and left.

5.2 LEFT on Belgum Trail; steep descent.

6.1 LEFT on Wildcat Creek Trail. *Water is available 0.5 mile to the right on Wildcat Creek Trail (Alvarado Staging Area).*

7.7 STRAIGHT at junction with Mezue Trail on left.

7.9 LEFT at junction with Havey Canyon Trail, then immediate RIGHT on Conlon Trail.

9.9 RIGHT on paved Nimitz Way.

11.3 Arrive at starting point.

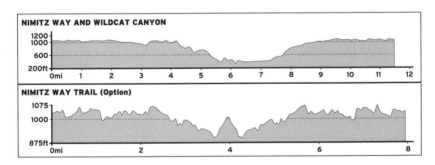

2 SKYLINE LOOP
Berkeley and Oakland hills

PAVED ROADS WITH MODERATE CAR TRAFFIC

Difficulty: 3   **Total Distance:** 28.5 miles (or 23-mile option)

Riding Time: 2 hours   **Elevation Gain:** 2,000 feet

Summary: This road ride travels past three of the East Bay hills' most popular parks, offering an abundance of San Francisco Bay views.

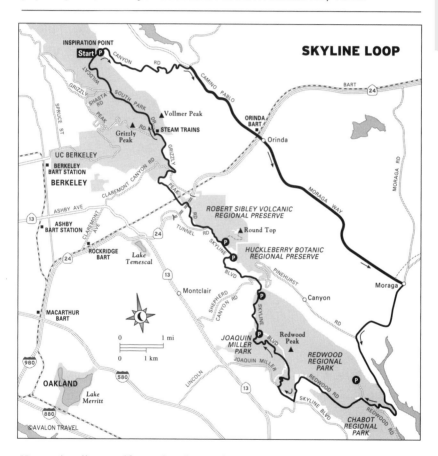

You can't call yourself a road cyclist in the San Francisco Bay Area until you've ridden the Skyline Loop in the East Bay hills. On a clear day, the loop's far-reaching views of San Francisco Bay, the cities of the East Bay, and Mount Diablo will knock your socks off. The route has just enough hills to provide a workout, but none are so steep that they are out of the range of possibility for most riders.

Far-reaching views of San Francisco Bay and the East Bay are seen from the Skyline Loop.

Plus, the roads have surprisingly little traffic, except for Moraga Way, which has a wide shoulder. All this and you can easily start the ride from Orinda, Moraga, Berkeley, or at one of several parks on Skyline Boulevard.

This route describes the loop starting from the Inspiration Point parking lot at Tilden Regional Park, a popular gathering place for cyclists on weekends and a great place to find a riding partner. (Get there early to procure a parking spot.) This trailhead choice means you begin your ride with a twisty descent and end with a twisty climb on Wildcat Canyon Road. But the ride has a multitude of climbs and descents, so you might as well get in the swing of things from the start.

The major hills are on Pinehurst Road, Skyline Boulevard, and Grizzly Peak Road. (The latter two roads are where you gain most of your bay views.) You also face a steep descent on South Park Drive, just after you pass the miniature steam train at Tilden Park, where families pay a few bucks to go for a 12-minute, open-air train tour. Keep your speed down as you descend on this moderately busy park road—not just to avoid cars, but also to avoid California newts: The cute brown and orange salamanders cross the road by the thousands each year during the rainy season. During the peak newt migration, South Park Drive is closed to cars, but open to cyclists.

Besides Tilden, this loop passes by two other East Bay regional parks: Redwood and Robert Sibley. Redwood is a popular spot for mountain biking and hiking. Sibley's main feature is Round Top Peak, the remains of an ancient volcano.

For more information about Tilden, Redwood, and Sibley Regional Parks,

contact East Bay Regional Park District, 510/635-0135 or 510/562-7275, www.
ebparks.org.

Options

For riders short on time, note the shortcut in the route directions at mile 10.9 on
Pinehurst Road. Turning right instead of left on Pinehurst will cut 5.5 miles off
the loop, but you'll face a steep climb up to Skyline Boulevard. The Pinehurst
shortcut does have its charms, however: The road sees almost no car traffic, is
lined with redwoods, and passes by the tiny hamlet of Canyon, with its one-room
schoolhouse and post office.

Driving Directions

From I-580 in Oakland, take Highway 24 east. Go through the Caldecott Tunnel
and exit at Orinda. Turn left on Camino Pablo. Drive north for 2 miles, then turn
left on Wildcat Canyon Road. Drive 2.4 miles to the Inspiration Point parking lot.

Route Directions

0.0 Park at Inspiration Point parking lot. Turn left out of the lot and
head downhill on Wildcat Canyon Road. *Supplies are available in
Berkeley or Orinda.*

2.4 RIGHT on Camino Pablo Road.

4.5 Cross under Highway 24; Camino Pablo becomes Moraga Way.

4.6 Arrive in Orinda. *Supplies are available.*

9.1 RIGHT on Canyon Road. *Supplies are available at the shopping center.*

10.9 LEFT on Pinehurst Road. *You can cut 5.5 miles off the loop by turning
right on Pinehurst Road here. After a steep climb, you'll rejoin the route
at mile 20.4, below, where you'll go straight onto Skyline.*

13.8 RIGHT on Redwood Road.

16.2 RIGHT on Skyline Boulevard.

16.8 RIGHT to stay on Skyline Boulevard at Joaquin Miller Road.

19.9 Redwood Regional Park Skyline gate. *Water is available.*

20.4 LEFT to stay on Skyline Boulevard at Pinehurst Road.

21.9 Robert Sibley Regional Preserve. *Water is available.*

22.0 RIGHT on Grizzly Peak Road.

24.4 STRAIGHT to stay on Grizzly Peak Road.

25.6 Tilden Regional Park's miniature steam train. *Water is available.*

25.8 RIGHT on South Park Drive.

27.3 RIGHT on Wildcat Canyon Road.

28.5 Arrive at starting point.

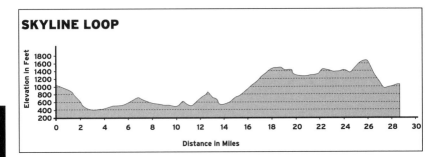

3 CARQUINEZ STRAIT LOOP
Martinez to Crockett

PAVED ROADS WITH MINIMAL CAR TRAFFIC

Difficulty: 2   **Total Distance:** 18.5 miles (or longer options)

Riding Time: 1.5-2 hours   **Elevation Gain:** 1,200 feet

Summary: One of the most interesting features of the San Francisco Bay waterway system, Carquinez Strait is the showpiece of this ride.

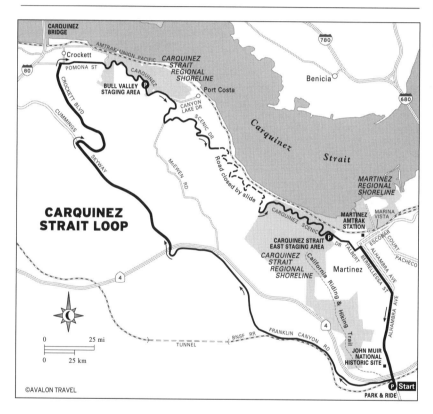

The northeastern arm of the conglomeration of waterways that constitute the bay and river delta, Carquinez Strait forms the narrow passageway between San Pablo and Suisun Bays. It's the meeting place of the Sacramento and San Joaquin Rivers, where they join together to flow to the Pacific Ocean through the Golden Gate.

Hundreds of thousands of king salmon once passed through here on their way to the Sacramento and San Joaquin Rivers to spawn. Native Americans lived off their abundance for centuries. In the 1800s, white settlers set up commercial fishing

Grasses and weeds push up through the broken pavement on this stretch of Carquinez Scenic Drive, which has been closed to cars since 1982.

operations and canneries along the strait; king salmon ruled the economy of this area. Today the only salmon you'll find in the towns of Martinez and Crockett are on dinner plates in homes and restaurants, but it is fascinating to recall the area's history as you ride this road tour between the two towns.

Due to events in more recent history, one portion of this road loop is closed to cars. A landslide in 1982 washed out a 1.7-mile-long section of Carquinez Scenic Drive. There's still enough road left for cyclists, but watch for broken pavement, gravel, and rocks. (You might want to ride your fat-tire bike here, or make sure you have a pair of Kevlar tire liners in your skinny tires.) It's easy to get distracted by the views overlooking Carquinez Strait, a wide expanse of blue waterway punctuated by the journeying of ships, large and small. As Carquinez Scenic Drive twists and turns, you gain ever-changing views of the Carquinez Bridge and the towns of Benecia and Vallejo.

Most of the climbing is accomplished in the first five miles of this ride (600-foot gain). The rest of the loop's ups are short, 200-foot-or-less climbs. There's also an exhilarating downhill on Crockett Boulevard into Crockett.

Options

For more views of the waterway, stop at Carquinez Strait Regional Shoreline just outside of Crockett and hike the one-mile Carquinez Overlook Loop Trail. Mountain bikers can also access the dirt California Riding and Hiking Trail from this ride's trailhead (the Park and Ride lot). Pedaling east, the trail connects to the paved Contra Costa Canal Trail in just under four miles. The Canal Trail then connects to the Iron Horse Regional Trail.

Driving Directions

From Walnut Creek, take I-680 north for six miles to Highway 4. Turn west on Highway 4 and drive three miles; take the Alhambra Avenue exit and drive south to the Park and Ride lot on the right.

Route Directions

0.0 Park at the Park and Ride lot at the junction of Alhambra Avenue and Franklin Canyon Road. Ride west on Franklin Canyon Road. *Supplies are available in Walnut Creek, Concord, or Martinez.*

4.4 RIGHT on Cummings Skyway.

6.5 RIGHT on Crockett Boulevard.

8.5 RIGHT on Pomona Street into downtown Crockett; Pomona Street becomes Carquinez Scenic Drive just outside of town. *Supplies are available in downtown Crockett.*

10.3 Carquinez Regional Strait Shoreline on the left (Bull Valley Staging Area). *You can lock up your bike and hike the one-mile Carquinez Overlook Loop Trail.*

12.5 Road closure; ride around the gate.

14.2 Road is open to cars again.

16.4 RIGHT on Talbart Street.

16.5 LEFT on Escobar Street.

16.6 RIGHT on Berrellessa Street (becomes Alhambra Avenue).

18.5 Arrive at starting point.

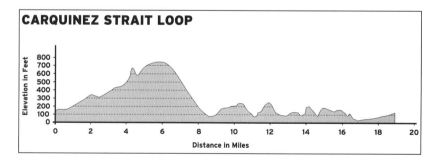

4 BRIONES CREST LOOP
Briones Regional Park near Orinda

DIRT ROAD AND SINGLE-TRACK

Difficulty: 2   **Total Distance:** 8 miles (or 13.5-mile option)

Riding Time: 1.5 hours   **Elevation Gain:** 1,200 feet

Summary: Ride through the grasslands and alongside the cows in an old Spanish land grant couched between three freeways.

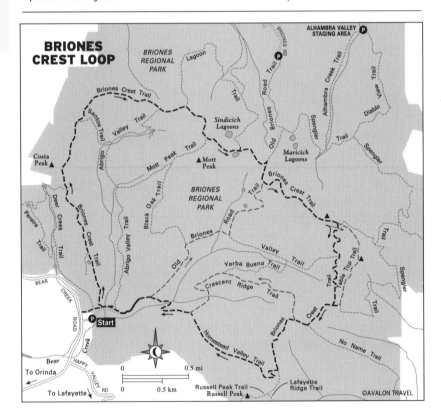

Briones Regional Park is nearly 6,000 acres of grasslands and oaks that was once part of Rancho San Felipe, a Spanish land grant. In the mid-1800s, it was an important fruit-growing region. Today it's the grassy home of grazing cows and is frequently visited by mountain bikers, dog walkers, hikers, and horseback riders.

The park is well known for its sunny exposure, numerous dirt roads, and large expanse of open grasslands. Bordered on three sides by freeways—Highway 4, I-680, and Highway 2—it's an oasis of open space in a heavily urbanized area.

Briones Regional Park contains nearly 6,000 acres of rolling grassland hills.

Because of an absence of shade in the park, summer is not the best time for a ride here. It can be as hot as Hades on July and August afternoons, although quite pleasant in winter, spring, and fall. Note that cows roam the Briones pasturelands, so as you ride you must pass through a number of cattle gates. And those same cows are notorious for rutting the heck out of the ranch roads, so expect a lot of bumps, especially noticeable on the downhills. Dual-suspension comes in handy here.

The first 0.5 mile of the Briones Crest Loop is on wide single-track and constitutes a grunt of a climb (three short hills with a total 400-foot elevation gain). But beyond that, the remaining hills are more moderate. Most of the ride is on wide ranch roads, which lend themselves to some fun downhills.

Don't forget to pause for a moment at mile 4.3, where you pass Briones Peak, the highest point in the park at 1,483 feet. The hilltop affords great views of mighty Mount Diablo.

For more information, contact East Bay Regional Park District, 510/635-0135 or 510/562-7275, www.ebparks.org.

Options

To extend your mileage and increase your workout, you can turn this ride into a double loop. Follow the route directions below to mile 7.7, then turn right on Old Briones Road. Travel 1.6 miles, then turn right on Briones Crest Trail (you'll pass Briones Peak again). Then, less than a mile later, go straight on Table Top Trail, heading for the radio antennas. In 0.8 mile, you'll be back on Briones Crest Trail. In another 0.5 mile, go right on Crescent Ridge Trail, pedaling past the archery range. You'll face a memorably steep descent. At 12.7 miles, go right on Homestead Valley Trail, then left on Old Briones Road 0.5 mile farther. This will take you back to the parking lot where you started your ride.

Driving Directions

From I-580 in Oakland, take Highway 24 east. Go through the Caldecott Tunnel and continue another 1.5 miles. Take the Orinda exit, then turn left on Camino Pablo and drive north for 2 miles. Turn right on Bear Creek Road and drive 4.4 miles, then turn right into the Briones Regional Park/Bear Creek Staging Area entrance. Turn left just past the kiosk and park in the lower parking lot.

Route Directions

0.0 Park in the lower parking lot at the Bear Creek Staging Area. The trailhead is at the end of the parking lot on the left. Follow Briones Crest Trail. *Water is available at the trailhead. Supplies are available in Orinda.*

0.1 RIGHT at Y-junction onto Briones Crest Trail.

0.5 End of the climb; trail widens and levels out.

1.1 STRAIGHT on Briones Crest Trail at junction with Deer Creek Trail. Stay straight on Briones Crest Trail at next four junctions.

3.3 Pass by Sindicich Lagoons (ranch ponds).

3.5 RIGHT on Old Briones Road.

3.6 LEFT on Briones Crest Trail.

4.3 Briones Peak, elevation 1,483 feet.

4.4 RIGHT to stay on Briones Crest Trail.

4.8 STRAIGHT on Briones Crest Trail.

5.7 STRAIGHT on Briones Crest Trail.

6.2 RIGHT on Homestead Valley Trail.

7.7 LEFT on Old Briones Road.

7.8 Go around gate and pass upper parking lot.

7.9 RIGHT at kiosk into lower parking lot.

8.0 Arrive at starting point.

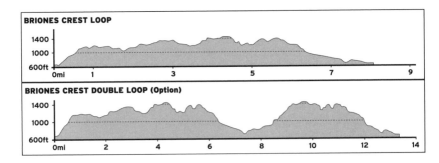

5 THREE BEARS LOOP
near San Pablo Reservoir and Orinda

PAVED ROADS WITH MODERATE CAR TRAFFIC

Difficulty: 3   **Total Distance:** 19.5 miles

Riding Time: 1.5 hours   **Elevation Gain:** 1,600 feet

Summary: A classic East Bay road ride, this loop cruises along bike lanes and wide road shoulders past San Pablo and Briones Reservoirs.

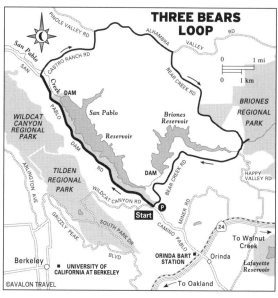

Every serious East Bay cyclist has his or her own version of the Three Bears ride, with a variety of starting points and mileage totals. But what all those rides have in common is a heart-pumping, aerobic "crank" up the triumvirate of hills on Bear Valley Road, affectionately known as Papa Bear, Mama Bear, and Baby Bear.

This is one of the shorter versions of that classic ride, perfect for after work or any time you want a workout on the bike without taking up a whole day. By starting and ending near downtown Orinda, you can complete the Three Bears Loop in just under 20 miles. The loop can be ridden in either direction. As it is described here, you face Mama Bear first (450-foot climb), Papa Bear second (500-foot climb), and save the easiest hill for last (only 100 feet for the Baby). In between, there is a rest stop at Briones Regional Park, where you can fill up your water bottles or have a seat at a shady picnic table.

Except for the first leg on busy San Pablo Dam Road and a short stretch through a cluster of red-tile-roofed subdivisions, most of the loop is on quiet back roads surrounded by open space. Bike lanes and wide shoulders make riding here stress-free. A highlight of this ride is its lovely views of two of the East Bay Municipal Utility District's reservoirs: San Pablo and Briones. In June, the roadside buckeye trees are in full bloom, wafting their sweet aroma through the air. The grasslands and chaparral plants emit their own pungent smell as they dry in the summer heat. You're far more likely to see quail and deer crossing the road than a parade of cars. This is the kind of pleasant ride you can do again and again, any time you're in the mood for a little exercise.

Driving Directions

From I-580 in Oakland, take Highway 24 east. Go through the Caldecott Tunnel and continue another 1.5 miles. Take the Orinda exit, then turn left on Camino Pablo and drive north for 2 miles. Turn right on Bear Creek Road and park in the pullout immediately on the left. (If this pullout is full, you can park in downtown Orinda, 1.6 miles south on Camino Pablo Road, then ride to this point.)

Route Directions

0.0 Park at the top of Bear Creek Road, near its junction with Camino Pablo/San Pablo Dam Road. Ride out to Camino Pablo/San Pablo Dam Road. *Supplies are available in Orinda.*

0.1 RIGHT on San Pablo Dam Road.

5.4 RIGHT on Castro Ranch Road.

7.6 RIGHT on Alhambra Valley Road.

10.4 RIGHT on Bear Creek Road.

11.9 Start up Mama Bear.

13.0 Top of Mama Bear.

14.3 LEFT at Briones Regional Park Bear Creek Staging Area. *Water is available.* TURN AROUND.

14.9 LEFT on Bear Creek Road.

15.2 Start up Papa Bear.

17.4 Top of Papa Bear.

18.9 Start up Baby Bear.

19.5 Arrive at starting point (top of Baby Bear).

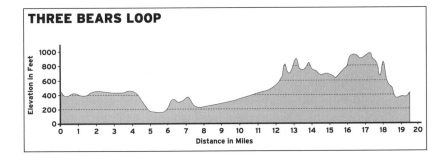

THREE BEARS LOOP

6 LAFAYETTE-MORAGA REGIONAL TRAIL
near Lafayette and Moraga

PAVED BIKE PATH

Difficulty: 1   **Total Distance:** 15.4 miles

Riding Time: 1.5 hours   **Elevation Gain:** 550 feet

Summary: This is a paved bike trail for every kind of rider, from first-timers on training wheels to East Bay bike commuters.

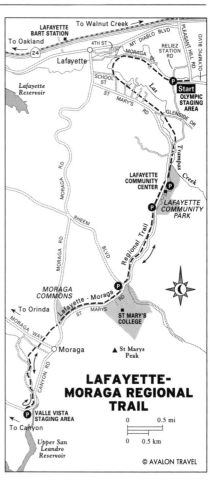

When suburbs grow so large that they connect town to town without any buffer of open land between them, one of the smartest things city planners can do is create spaces where people can get a little fresh air and sunshine—places protected from cars, traffic, and urban noise. The Lafayette–Moraga Trail is such a place, and it is used by more than half a million people per year.

It's not exactly a trip to the wilderness, but you will see plenty of squirrels along the trail—not plain old Bay Area gray squirrels, but cute and chubby red squirrels with shiny, rust-colored coats. I spotted some busily burying nuts in flower beds, their genetic instinct preparing them for the long, hard, snowbound winter that will never come to sunny Moraga.

Also in the cute category, it's not uncommon to see an entire pack of Cub Scouts ride by, dressed in their smart navy blue uniforms and tiny bicycle helmets. That's the kind of trail this is. A stretch of the old San Francisco–Sacramento Railroad, the path retains some of its railroad history with white crossing signs proudly displayed at junctions around Lafayette.

On the negative side, Lafayette–Moraga Trail is intersected by several roads.

The Lafayette-Moraga Regional Trail was opened in 1976 as one of the first 500 converted rail trails in the United States.

Only one, St. Mary's Road, is likely to have much traffic. Beyond this crossing, you leave most of the neighborhoods behind and see less of St. Mary's Road (which parallels the trail up to this crossing). The trail passes St. Mary's College, which has a pretty white church tower set in the hillside and is surrounded by green playing fields. Shortly thereafter is Moraga Commons, a town park with a play area, restrooms, par course, and the like. A waterfall sculpture is located near a sign noting that the Lafayette–Moraga Trail was opened in 1976 as one of America's first 500 rail trails. The trail's final stretch leads out to the country, ending at the Valle Vista Staging Area on Canyon Road, where you simply turn around and head back.

For more information, contact East Bay Regional Park District, 510/635-0135 or 510/562-7275, www.ebparks.org.

Options

If you're a fan of paved recreation trails in the East Bay, you must take a ride on the Iron Horse Regional Trail, which runs between the cities of Concord and Dublin, following the Southern Pacific Railroad right-of-way established in 1891. When completed, the Iron Horse Trail will stretch 55 miles from Livermore in Alameda County to Suisun Bay in Contra Costa County, connecting 12 cities. Currently about 30 miles of trail are accessible. For more information and a trail map, go to www.ebparks.org.

Driving Directions

From I-580 in Oakland, take Highway 24 east toward Walnut Creek. Go through the Caldecott Tunnel and take the Pleasant Hill Road exit south. Drive 0.7 mile to Olympic Boulevard and turn right. The parking lot is on the right in about 50 yards.

Route Directions

0.0 Park at Olympic Staging Area. *Water is available along the trail.*

1.1 STRAIGHT at junction with Briones-to-Mount Diablo Trail.

3.3 Cross St. Mary's Road.

3.4 Lafayette Community Center. *Water is available.*

5.2 St. Mary's College campus.

6.0 Moraga Commons park. *Water is available.*

7.7 Valle Vista Staging Area. TURN AROUND.

15.4 Arrive at starting point.

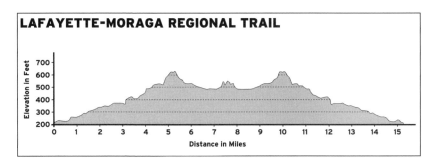

⑦ STEWARTVILLE AND RIDGE TRAILS LOOP

Black Diamond Mines Regional Preserve near Antioch

DIRT ROAD

Difficulty: 3   **Total Distance:** 10.8 miles

Riding Time: 2 hours   **Elevation Gain:** 1,900 feet

Summary: A little-known slice of East Bay history is revealed at this mountain bike-friendly East Bay regional park.

From 1860 to 1906, the Mount Diablo Coal Field was the largest coal mining district in California. Located in what is now Black Diamond Mines Regional Preserve, this productive coal field on the northern side of Mount Diablo prompted the digging of 12 major mines and the growth of five townships. Much of this mining history, and a large acreage of rolling grassland hills and chaparral-clad slopes, is preserved at Black Diamond Mines.

This loop ride reveals some of the park's highlights and adds some heart-pumping, leg-burning exercise to the bargain. Start with a mind-expanding trip to the park's Greathouse Visitor Center, which has been closed for many years for structural improvements but is scheduled to reopen in summer 2012, then pedal the level Railroad Bed Trail to Stewartville Trail. A 0.5-mile ascent brings you to

Ride through grassy valleys and steep hills on the Stewartville and Ridge Trails Loop.

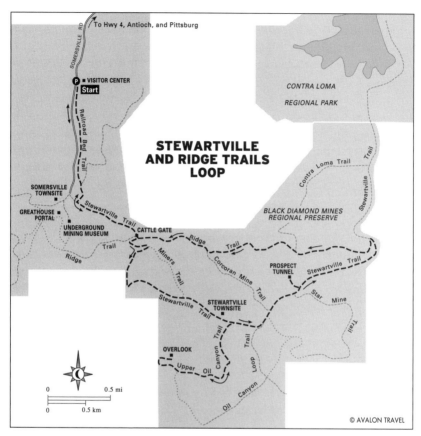

To Hwy 4, Antioch, and Pittsburg

SOMERSVILLE RD

■ VISITOR CENTER
Start

Railroad Bed Trail

CONTRA LOMA
REGIONAL PARK

**STEWARTVILLE
AND RIDGE TRAILS
LOOP**

Contra Loma Trail

Stewartville Trail

SOMERSVILLE
TOWNSITE

GREATHOUSE
PORTAL ■

UNDERGROUND
MINING MUSEUM ■

Stewartville Trail

CATTLE GATE

Ridge   Trail

BLACK DIAMOND MINES
REGIONAL PRESERVE

Trail

Ridge

Miners   Trail

Corcoran Mine Trail

PROSPECT
TUNNEL

Stewartville Trail

Star   Mine

Trail

Stewartville
Trail

STEWARTVILLE
TOWNSITE

Canyon   Trail

Loop

Oil   Canyon

OVERLOOK ■

Upper   Oil

0   0.5 mi

0   0.5 km

© AVALON TRAVEL

a cattle gate at a high point. Pass through the gate and admire the deep, grassy valley below you. The good news is that you're going to ride into that pretty valley; the bad news is that you'll have to climb back out of it.

Don't miss two spurs off the loop: Upper Oil Canyon Trail, which leads steeply uphill to an overlook of the valley, and Tunnel Trail to Prospect Tunnel, an obvious gaping hole in the hillside. You can explore about 150 feet into the dark, cool mine shaft before you reach a steel gate. The shaft was driven in the 1860s by miners in search of coal, or "black diamonds."

A mile past Tunnel Trail, make a sharp left turn on Ridge Trail, leaving the valley and beginning a steep, two-mile-long ascent. Ridge Trail rollercoasters along, dipping down occasionally but more often rising on very steep grades (steep enough that you may be forced to walk your bike). The painful climb is eased by the sudden appearance of views to the north of Carquinez Strait, Suisun Bay, Pittsburg, and Antioch. Pause to enjoy the vistas while you catch your breath.

When at last Ridge Trail returns you to the gate at Stewartville Trail, consider a rest on the bench by the gate, where you can admire the rolling terrain you just explored. Then it's an easy 1.4 miles back to your car.

Because there is no technical single-track on this ride, it may be tempting to bring beginning mountain bikers here. But unless they are very fit and ambitious, the many short but steep ascents may break their spirit. All riders should stay away from this park's trails when they are wet; the place is famous for its clay-like mud, which can bring your wheels to a dead standstill, even on the downhills.

For more information, contact East Bay Regional Park District, 510/635-0135 or 510/562-7275, www.ebparks.org. Black Diamond Mines Regional Preserve (510/544-2750) is located at 5175 Somersville Road in Antioch.

Options

If a ride around this park whets your appetite for more information on this area's mining history, consider taking a tour of the silica-producing Hazel-Atlas Mine at Black Diamond Mines Regional Preserve. The guided one-hour tour travels 400 feet back into the mine tunnel so participants can see the office of the mine boss, ore chutes, and other features. Tickets for the tour ($5 per person) can be purchased at the park visitor center. Tours are offered on weekends only, March–November, at noon and 3 P.M.

Driving Directions

From Highway 4 in Antioch, take the Somersville Road exit south. Drive three miles south on Somersville Road to the parking lot by the visitor center.

Route Directions

0.0 Park by the visitor center on Somersville Road. Take Railroad Bed Trail from the southern end of the parking lot. *Water is available at the visitor center; supplies are available in Antioch.*

0.7 LEFT on Stewartville Trail.

1.4 Cattle gate and viewpoint. Go through gate, then RIGHT to stay on Stewartville Trail; steep descent.

1.8 RIGHT at junction with Miners Trail to stay on Stewartville Trail.

3.2 RIGHT on Upper Oil Canyon Trail.

4.4 Arrive at overlook. TURN AROUND.

5.6 RIGHT to continue on Stewartville Trail.

6.1 LEFT on Tunnel Trail. Park your bike and walk into the dark tunnel, then TURN AROUND.

6.4 LEFT to continue on Stewartville Trail.

7.3 LEFT (very sharp turn) on Ridge Trail; steep climb begins.

9.4 RIGHT on Stewartville Trail at cattle gate.
10.1 RIGHT on Railroad Bed Trail.
10.8 Arrive at starting point.

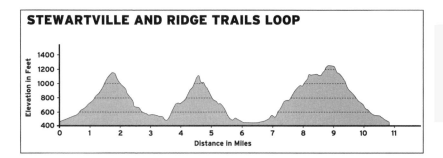

STEWARTVILLE AND RIDGE TRAILS LOOP

8 EAST AND WEST RIDGE LOOP
Redwood Regional Park near Oakland

DIRT ROAD

Difficulty: 2   **Total Distance:** 9.4 miles

Riding Time: 2 hours   **Elevation Gain:** 1,100 feet

Summary: Just a few minutes from downtown Oakland lie dense groves of redwood trees, an observatory and planetarium, and one of the East Bay's most popular mountain biking trails.

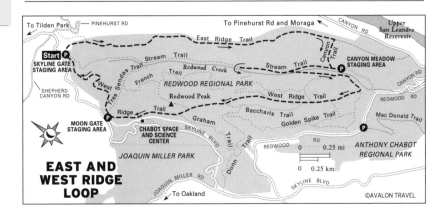

They don't call this place Redwood Regional Park for nothing. The dark, shaggy-barked trees grow more than 100 feet tall, and their shady canopy covers a vast expanse of the park. The redwoods are the second-generation offspring of the original trees that once towered over this canyon. Between 1840 and 1860, loggers felled these ancient giants to provide lumber for the growing cities of San Francisco and San Jose.

The redwoods aren't the only prizes of Redwood Regional Park. The park is bordered by two high ridges to the east and west, both of which offer expansive views. This loop ride, a standard for East Bay mountain bikers, travels outward on East Ridge and back on West Ridge. Although the ride is entirely on wide dirt roads, it still presents some technical challenges, particularly on a steep, rutted downhill on Canyon Trail and a steep uphill on West Ridge Trail. Strong beginners should be able to handle it, or at least walk their bikes if they can't.

From the Skyline Gate Staging Area, follow East Ridge Trail generally downhill for 3 miles in a two-steps-down, one-step-up fashion, rolling along small hills. Watch for long-distance views of the reservoirs to the east. Turn right on Canyon Trail, drop steeply, then follow Stream Trail into the canyon for an up close look

ANN MARIE BROWN

West Ridge Trail at Redwood Regional Park offers views of Oakland and San Francisco Bay to the west and Mount Diablo to the east.

at some of the park's redwood stands. After a brief, level out-and-back on Stream Trail, you'll face a hardy climb on West Ridge Trail. The first 0.75 mile is the worst (400-foot gain), but the trail continues to ascend moderately for almost 3 miles.

West Ridge Trail's final stretch passes by the observatory at the Chabot Space and Science Center (worth a visit; see *Options*). You'll catch fine glimpses of Oakland and San Francisco Bay to the west; equally good is the view to the east of looming Mount Diablo at 3,849 feet. The last mile is a delightfully easy cruise back to Skyline Gate through a shady forest of bay laurel, madrone, and Monterey pine.

For more information, contact East Bay Regional Park District, 510/635-0135 or 510/562-7275, www.ebparks.org.

Options

Combine this ride with a visit to the Chabot Space and Science Center. The center keeps a watch on the stars, including 9,100 of a simulated variety, which appear daily on the planetarium's 70-foot domed ceiling. Peer through massive telescopes, admire a moon rock, sit in a replica of the Mercury space capsule, or ponder the Milky Way while you nosh at the Celestial Cafe. Visit www.chabotspace.org for more information. Hours are 10 A.M.–5 P.M. Wednesday–Thursday, 10 A.M.–10 P.M. Friday–Saturday, and 10 A.M.–5 P.M. Sunday.

Driving Directions

From I-580 in Oakland, take the 35th Avenue exit and turn north. Drive 2.4 miles

(35th Avenue will become Redwood Road). Turn left on Skyline Boulevard and drive 3.7 miles to the Skyline Gate Staging Area, located at the intersection of Skyline and Pine Hills Drive. (Skyline Boulevard makes a sharp right turn after the first 0.5 mile.)

Route Directions

0.0 Park at Skyline Gate Staging Area and take East Ridge Trail, the northernmost of three possible trails. *Water is available at the trailhead.*

2.9 RIGHT on Canyon Trail.

3.3 RIGHT on Stream Trail at Canyon Meadow Staging Area.

3.6 STRAIGHT at junction with Bridle Trail; you'll return to this intersection shortly.

4.2 End of bikes-allowed section of Stream Trail. TURN AROUND. *Stop at one of five picnic areas under the redwoods. Water is available.*

4.8 RIGHT on Bridle Trail upon return to previous junction.

5.0 RIGHT on West Ridge Trail; begin ascent to ridge.

6.3 RIGHT to stay on West Ridge Trail.

7.7 Chabot Space and Science Center.

9.4 Arrive at starting point.

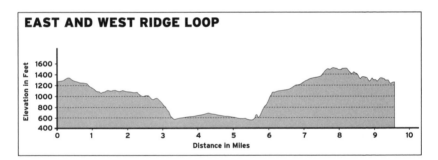

9 WALL POINT AND BARBEQUE TERRACE LOOP

Mount Diablo State Park near Danville

DIRT ROADS

Difficulty: 3   **Total Distance:** 9.4 miles

Riding Time: 2 hours   **Elevation Gain:** 1,600 feet

Summary: This challenging dirt loop on the Devil's Mountain, 3,849-foot Mount Diablo includes a visit to *Flintstones*-inspired Rock City.

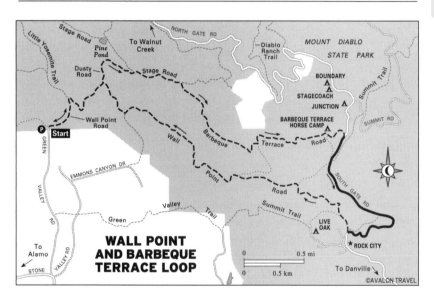

Ride the Devil. That's the attitude of most mountain bikers who come to pedal on "devilish" Mount Diablo. The great 3,849-foot peak is a butt-kicker for casual riders, due to steep and rugged fire roads, occasional stretches of single-track that require advanced technical skills, and the brutally hot temperatures that occur on these slopes during 4–5 months of the year. That said, the Wall Point and Barbeque Terrace Loop is one of the more manageable rides on the mountain, although it certainly has its share of ups and downs.

The trip starts at the Macedo Ranch trailhead and begins with a moderate climb up Wall Point Road. This is followed by a rocky descent into Pine Canyon, which may present some technical challenges to the less experienced. This downhill is known as "the staircase" because of its layers of exposed rock. Pine Canyon is especially lovely in winter when its stream flows, but the wet season also

A tough climb on Barbeque Terrace Road leads to a rewarding view looking out over Pine Canyon.

necessitates a few creek crossings. After a series of heavy storms, Pine Canyon can even become impassable. Call the park to check on trail conditions if you are visiting in the winter or early spring.

A tough climb ensues on Barbeque Terrace Road out of Pine Canyon, in which you must gain 900 feet in little more than a mile, often on a loose, pebbly surface. After that difficult ascent, which leaves many riders walking their bikes and weeping in the Diablo dust, the trail ends at Barbeque Terrace Group Campground. Admire the view from the trail gate and congratulate yourself for having made it up this hellacious hill. Then ride up the paved camp access road to South Gate Road for a fast downhill on pavement to Rock City. (A short single-track option is also possible here.)

Lock up your bike and take a brief walk at Rock City. Set among clusters of tall manzanita, foothill pines, madrones, and live oaks, Rock City is a jumble of eroded sandstone outcroppings that was formed 40 or 50 million years ago during the Eocene period, when Mount Diablo was buried under a great sea. Eventually the waters receded and the remaining sand hardened into a ridge of rocks. This rocky ridge has been weathered and eroded by centuries of wind and rain, creating odd-shaped boulders with small caves and Swiss cheese–style holes. They're fun to look at and climb around on.

After exploring the rocks, loop back to Macedo Ranch on Wall Point Road, a wide fire road that runs along a rocky ridgeline. As you pedal west, you'll have lovely views of Rock City and two concrete cities—Danville and Walnut Creek—to the west. You'll face a moderate climb for the first 1.6 miles, then it's downhill all the way back to the parking lot.

For more information, contact Mount Diablo State Park, 925/837-2525 or 925/837-0904, www.mdia.org or www.parks.ca.gov.

Driving Directions

From I-680 at Danville, take the Diablo Road exit and head east. Follow Diablo Road for 1.4 miles (turn right at 0.7 mile to stay on Diablo Road), then turn left at Green Valley Road. Drive 2 miles to the end of Green Valley Road and the Macedo Ranch trailhead.

Route Directions

0.0 Park at Macedo Ranch and start riding on the fire road by the signboard and water trough. This is Wall Point Road, but it is signed as Macedo Ranch to Summit Trail. *Supplies are available in Danville.*

0.3 RIGHT to stay on Wall Point Road.

0.9 LEFT on Dusty Road/Pine Canyon Trail (Wall Point Road goes right).

1.4 RIGHT on Stage Road.

1.8 RIGHT on Barbeque Terrace Road.

2.6 Tough climb begins.

3.7 Barbecue Terrace Group Campground; follow paved camp road uphill to paved South Gate Road. *Water is available at the group camp.*

4.0 RIGHT on South Gate Road. *If you prefer to ride on dirt, you can pick up single-track Summit Trail 0.2 mile down South Gate Road on the right, signed as Multi-Purpose Trail.*

5.7 RIGHT at Rock City/Live Oak parking lot. *Lock up your bike and explore the fascinating rocks.* TURN AROUND. Ride 50 yards uphill (backtracking) on South Gate Road to the start of Wall Point Road (across from the private residence and service area).

5.8 LEFT on Wall Point Road. *Water is available at the service area across from the start of Wall Point Road.*

8.3 RIGHT to stay on Wall Point Road.

8.5 LEFT to stay on Wall Point Road.

9.4 Arrive at starting point.

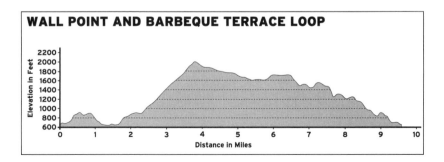

WALL POINT AND BARBEQUE TERRACE LOOP

10 MITCHELL AND DONNER CANYONS LOOP

Mount Diablo State Park near Clayton

DIRT ROADS AND SINGLE-TRACK

Difficulty: 4   **Total Distance:** 13.1 miles (or 8.6-mile option)

Riding Time: 2.5 hours   **Elevation Gain:** 2,900 feet

Summary: Tricky single-track, challenging climbs, and a variety of close-up and far-off scenery await riders on the back side of Mount Diablo.

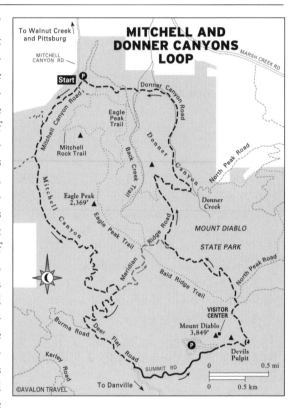

This ride on the "back" (north) side of Mount Diablo isn't particularly long, but it is quite strenuous. Still, the rewards are great: The loop passes by some of the most diverse habitats that the old Devil's Mountain has to offer, including gangly Coulter and foothill pines with their heavyweight cones, a wide range of chaparral plants (sage, toyon, manzanita, yerba santa, and more) and lush streamside vegetation. Plus, with the completion of every gut-thumping ascent on this route, you are rewarded with wide views of the surrounding area.

Mitchell Canyon Fire Road starts out deceptively easy, with a gentle climb along Mitchell Creek. But just past the two-mile mark, things start to get ugly—I mean, challenging. Over the next stretch to Deer Flat, you'll gain 1,200 feet, much of it with average grades that reach into the mid-teens and almost no shade from the ruthless sun. If you are crying uncle by the time you reach Deer Flat, check out the *Options* section. Meanwhile, the intrepid rider will continue on a 1,000-foot

Make sure you choose a cool day for riding the shadeless stretches of the Mitchell and Donner Canyons Loop.

climb to Juniper Campground and the paved Summit Road, then climb some more, this time on blessedly smooth pavement, to a 3,400-foot-high point called the Devils Elbow.

Here, single-track lovers will be thrilled by North Peak Trail's one mile of technically tricky stuff, which throws plenty of rocks and tree roots in your path as it makes a speedy descent to a saddle at Prospectors Gap. This is a good place to repeat to yourself the Smart Mountain Biker's Mantra: "Caution is the better part of valor." It is also a good place to slow down and enjoy the views, which extend southwest to the windmills in Livermore and east to the Central Valley. You'll pass directly below the large rock outcrop called Devils Pulpit on Mount Diablo's summit.

At the saddle at Prospectors Gap, you'll follow yet another fire road very steeply downhill until you meet up with Meridian Ridge Road and then Meridian Point, an overlook with a wide view of Clayton and a glimpse at Suisun Bay to the northwest. Then it's onward to Donner Canyon Road, Murchio Road, and back to the trailhead at Mitchell Canyon.

For more information, contact Mount Diablo State Park, 925/837-2525 or 925/837-0904, www.mdia.org or www.parks.ca.gov.

Options

If you've had enough when you reach oak-shaded Deer Flat, you can always bail out and head back on Meridian Ridge Road, making an 8.6-mile loop with only a 0.5-mile additional ascent. By choosing this option, you can add a thrilling short hike to your day. Lock up your bike near Murchio Gap on Meridian Ridge Road and walk out and back on the Eagle Peak Trail to Eagle Peak, elevation 2,369 feet. The 0.8-mile-long trail leads along the narrow backbone of Bald Ridge, with steep drop-offs on both sides. From Eagle Peak's rocky summit, you'll gain wide vistas of Mount Diablo's North Peak, the Sacramento and San Joaquin Delta, Honker Bay, and Suisun Bay. Although you opted for the shorter bike ride, after visiting this impressive summit you can call yourself a real mountaineer.

Driving Directions

From I-680 heading north in Walnut Creek, take the Ygnacio Valley Road exit. Drive east on Ygnacio Valley Road for 7.5 miles to Clayton Road. Turn right (south) on Clayton Road and drive 1.5 miles to Mitchell Canyon Road. Turn right and drive to the end of the road and the trailhead.

Route Directions

0.0 Park at the Mitchell Canyon trailhead and begin riding on Mitchell Canyon Fire Road. *Supplies are available in Clayton.*

2.0 Begin serious climb.

3.8 RIGHT on Deer Flat Road at Deer Flat (three-way junction).

4.9 LEFT to stay on Deer Flat Road at junction with Burma Road.

5.4 Juniper Campground; follow the paved camp road out to Summit Road. *Water is available at Juniper Campground.*

5.6 LEFT on paved Summit Road.

7.1 RIGHT on North Peak Trail (single-track) at hairpin turn in road (Devils Elbow).

8.1 LEFT on Prospectors Gap Road.

9.4 RIGHT on Meridian Ridge Road.

10.8 LEFT on Donner Canyon Road at junction with Cardinet Oaks Road.

12.1 LEFT on Murchio Road; stay straight at next three junctions.

13.1 Arrive at starting point.

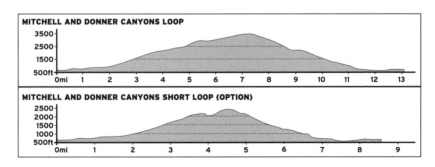

11 MOUNT DIABLO SUMMIT RIDE   BEST (

Blackhawk to Mount Diablo summit

PAVED ROADS WITH MODERATE CAR TRAFFIC

Difficulty: 4   **Total Distance:** 29.6 miles

Riding Time: 4-5 hours   **Elevation Gain:** 3,200 feet

Summary: Pick a clear day – preferably the day after a winter storm – for a ride up Mount Diablo to its rewarding panoramic summit view.

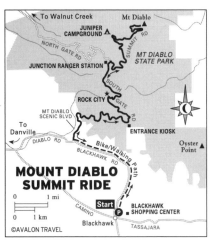

Almost everybody thinks about making the trip to 3,849-foot Mount Diablo from time to time. After all, you see it from just about everywhere in the Bay Area. It's not the tallest mountain around San Francisco Bay (Mount Hamilton near San Jose is 360 feet taller), but it has a way of making its presence known, looming in the background of the lives of millions of East Bay residents.

Although most people travel to the summit of Mount Diablo by car, a better way to get there is by bike. Sure, the ride is a long grind with a nearly nonstop elevation gain, but this is what you live for, right? You haven't really experienced Diablo's Summit Road until you've ridden it on a bike. With every curve in the winding pavement, the views are constantly changing.

Two roads—North Gate and South Gate—travel most of the way up the mountain; they join at Junction Ranger Station for the final 4.5 miles on Summit Road to the top. This ride follows South Gate Road from Blackhawk, elevation 738 feet; it's the easier of the two roads. Okay, full disclosure: It's only slightly easier. But when you take in the remarkable view from Diablo's summit, it's all worth it. On the clearest days, it's easy to spot the Farallon Islands, Lick Observatory on Mount Hamilton, Mount St. Helena in Calistoga, and even Mount Lassen to the north and the Sierra Nevada to the east. Bar none, it's the best view from any single spot in the East Bay.

Pick a cool day (forget summer on this shadeless "devil's mountain") and be encouraged by the fact that water and rest stops are plentiful all the way up the mountain (most roadside picnic areas and campgrounds have water).

With every curve in the winding pavement that leads to the summit of Mount Diablo, the vistas are constantly changing.

For more information, contact Mount Diablo State Park, 925/837-2525 or 925/837-0904, www.mdia.org or www.parks.ca.gov.

Options

If you want to shorten this ride, just drive your car farther up the mountain road and start from one of the parking areas within the state park, such as Curry Point or Rock City. And when you get to the summit of Mount Diablo, be sure to stop in at the Summit Museum (open 10 A.M.–4 P.M. daily, 925/837-6119, www.mdia.org/museum), a historic stone building that was built in the 1930s from sandstone blocks quarried in the park. The museum features permanent exhibits on the mountain's geology, natural history, and Native American history, as well as rotating art exhibits and an observation deck with telescopes.

Driving Directions

From the junction of I-680 and I-580 in Dublin, drive north on I-680 for five miles to the Crow Canyon Road exit. Drive east for four miles; Crow Canyon Road becomes Blackhawk Road at its junction with Tassajara Road. Park at or near the Blackhawk Plaza shopping center.

Route Directions

0.0 Park at or near Blackhawk Plaza shopping center and ride east on

Blackhawk Road, then pick up the bike/walking path alongside the road. *Supplies are available at the shopping center.*

3.4 RIGHT on Mount Diablo Scenic Boulevard.

4.5 Mount Diablo State Park gate.

7.1 Entrance kiosk; road changes names to South Gate Road.

7.6 Rock City region of the park.

8.2 Rock City parking area (good alternate starting point).

8.8 Curry Point parking area.

10.3 RIGHT on Summit Road at Junction Ranger Station.

12.8 Juniper Campground.

14.8 Mount Diablo summit and Summit Museum. TURN AROUND.

29.6 Arrive at starting point.

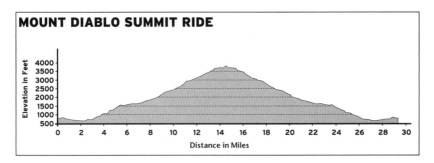

MOUNT DIABLO SUMMIT RIDE

12 ROUND VALLEY RAMBLE
Round Valley Regional Preserve near Clayton

DIRT ROAD

Difficulty: 1   **Total Distance:** 10.8 miles (or longer options)

Riding Time: 1.5 hours   **Elevation Gain:** 600 feet

Summary: A gentle ride through the Clayton countryside, this route is ideal for a spring day when the grasses are green and the wildflowers are blooming.

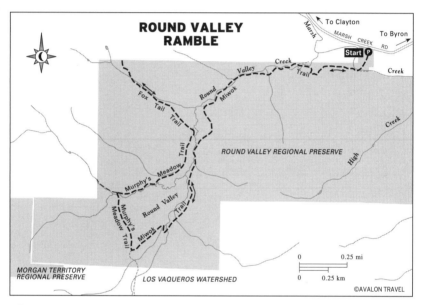

If you ever start to feel like the East Bay is too crowded, too congested, and has too much concrete, take a trip a little farther east to the northeast side of Mount Diablo. Here on the far eastern edge of the San Francisco Bay Area are wide-open spaces, spring wildflowers, and stately oak trees.

You'll find all this and more at Round Valley Regional Preserve, the 2,000-acre home of nesting golden eagles, burrowing owls, chubby ground squirrels, and the endangered San Joaquin kit fox. The bike riding here is mellow and easy, unless of course you show up at midday in August, when it can be more than 100 degrees.

From the preserve staging area, the trail starts out with a long bridge over Marsh Creek. At the far side of the bridge, a right turn puts you on Miwok Trail. Immediately you face the only real hill of the day; the remaining miles of this ride are mostly level.

The pastoral landscape of Round Valley makes for a pleasant ride and a chance for solitude.

In 0.5 mile, the wide dirt road meets up with Round Valley Creek. If you've timed your trip for the wet season, the stream will run cool and clear alongside you for much of your ride. You'll notice the remains of old farming equipment along the dirt trail; this land was farmed by the Murphy family from 1873 until 1988, when it was donated to the East Bay Regional Park District.

Stay on Miwok Trail through the entire length of the preserve, then turn right on Murphy's Meadow Trail. You'll loop back on the far side of Round Valley Creek. At a junction with Fox Tail Trail, follow Fox Tail uphill for a short out-and-back excursion. Head for the top of the hill, where you'll find a wide view of rolling hills and vast, unpopulated parkland. What a fine spot for a picnic lunch. When you've finished your meal, just turn around and retrace your tire treads back to your car.

Free maps available from the East Bay Regional Park District (510/562-7275 or 510/635-0135, www.ebparks.org) can get you where you want to go.

Options

Riders looking for more mileage can follow Miwok Trail out of the park, through a 1.6-mile stretch of Los Vaqueros Watershed, and into the east side of Morgan Territory Regional Preserve, where most trails are open to mountain bikes (see ride 13, *Volvon and Valley View Loop*).

Driving Directions

From I-580 in Livermore, take the Vasco Road exit and drive north 13 miles. Turn left (west) on Camino Diablo Road and drive 3.5 miles. Where Camino Diablo ends, continue straight on Marsh Creek Road for 1.5 miles to the Round Valley parking area on the left.

Route Directions

0.0 Park at Round Valley Staging Area and ride across the bridge. *Supplies are available in Clayton, eight miles west.*

0.1 RIGHT on Miwok Trail at far side of bridge.

0.5 STRAIGHT at junction with trail on right.

2.8 RIGHT on Murphy's Meadow Trail. *Miwok Trail leaves the park here and travels through the Los Vaqueros Watershed and into Morgan Territory Regional Preserve, for more riding options.*

3.7 RIGHT to stay on Murphy's Meadow Trail.

4.6 LEFT on Fox Tail Trail.

5.4 End of Fox Tail Trail. TURN AROUND.

10.8 Arrive at starting point.

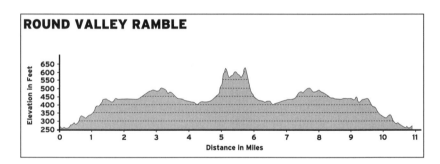

ROUND VALLEY RAMBLE

13 VOLVON AND VALLEY VIEW LOOP

Morgan Territory Regional Preserve near Livermore

DIRT ROAD

Difficulty: 3   **Total Distance:** 8.4 miles

Riding Time: 2 hours   **Elevation Gain:** 1,200 feet

Summary: The Old West is still alive at this preserve on the far eastern edge of the East Bay, where cattle and horses roam among grasslands and oaks.

Morgan Territory—even this park's name sounds wild, like a holdover from the Old West. If you're wondering if anything wild might still exist in Contra Costa County, wonder no more. Come to Morgan Territory and rediscover the wild East Bay.

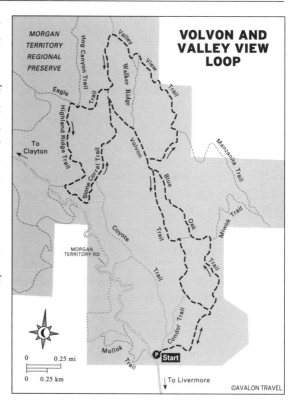

The drive to the trailhead is a trip in itself. You'll follow narrow, winding Morgan Territory Road north of Livermore to the preserve's main trailhead. Try not to get so wowed by the views that you drive right off the curvy, narrow road.

At the trailhead parking lot, you've climbed to 1,900 feet in elevation. (Okay, so your car has done the work.) Hopefully you've planned your visit for the cooler months of the year, because the open hills around Livermore bake in the summer. If you're riding in the warm season, make sure it is *very* early in the morning. Pick up a free trail map at the trailhead (the preserve has an overabundance of trail junctions) and follow Volvon Trail uphill and through a cattle gate.

Morgan Territory's rolling hills are punctuated by magnificent oak trees and colorful spring wildflowers.

Successive trails—Volvon, Blue Oak, and Valley View—carry you up and down Morgan Territory's scenic, rolling hills, which are punctuated by magnificent oak trees and colorful lichen-coated rocks. In the spring, more than 90 wildflower species blossom along these grassy hillsides. Views to the west of Mount Diablo are fine, but what is most surprising is Valley View Trail's eastern perspective on the San Joaquin Valley. On the clearest days of winter, the snowcapped High Sierra can be seen, more than 100 miles away.

The route described makes a dogleg from Valley View to cruise a section of 1,700-foot Highland Ridge, where more views are yours for the taking. The final stretch of the route is a long, mostly level cruise back to the trailhead on Volvon Trail. Overall, the riding is generally easy here, with wide trails and few technical challenges except for the ruts and holes caused by the trampling feet of cattle. You'll probably see a few groups of cud-chewing bovines somewhere along the path. They usually flee from mountain bikers, or stop in mid-chew to stare at you.

For more information, contact East Bay Regional Park District, 510/635-0135 or 510/562-7275, www.ebparks.org.

Driving Directions

From I-580 in Livermore, take the North Livermore Avenue exit and turn north. Drive north for 4 miles, then turn right on Morgan Territory Road. Drive 5.6 miles to the entrance to Morgan Territory Preserve on the right. (The road is narrow and steep.)

Route Directions

0.0 Park at Morgan Territory Preserve trailhead. Start riding on the main, wide trail (Volvon Trail). *Supplies are available in Livermore; stock up before you drive out Morgan Territory Road.*

0.3 LEFT, then immediately RIGHT on Blue Oak Trail.

1.7 STRAIGHT on Volvon Trail.

1.8 RIGHT on Valley View Trail.

3.0 RIGHT on Volvon Loop Trail.

3.7 RIGHT on Eagle Trail.

4.1 LEFT on Highland Ridge Trail.

5.0 LEFT on Stone Corral Trail just before Highland Ridge Trail meets paved road.

6.1 RIGHT on Volvon Trail; stay on Volvon Trail at the next several junctions.

8.0 RIGHT, then immediately RIGHT again to stay on Volvon Trail.

8.4 Arrive at starting point.

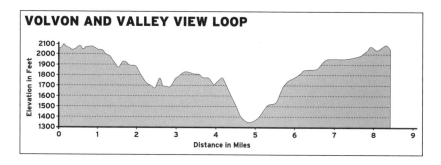

VOLVON AND VALLEY VIEW LOOP

14 LAKE CHABOT LOOP
Lake Chabot and Anthony Chabot Regional Parks, east of San Leandro

DIRT ROAD AND PAVED BIKE PATH

Difficulty: 3   **Total Distance:** 13.3 miles (or 9-mile option)

Riding Time: 2 hours   **Elevation Gain:** 1,200 feet

Summary: This is a great training ride for East Bay mountain bikers looking to sharpen their skills, and an easy paved route around the lakeshore for families and those on skinny tires.

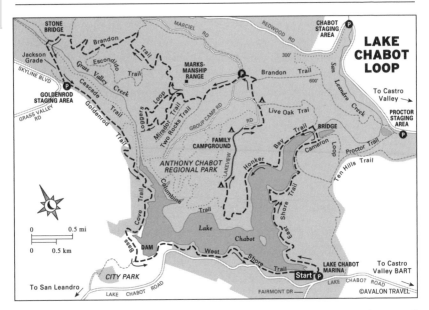

Lakeside trails are often level and somewhat predictable, but the trails around Lake Chabot never stop turning, twisting, climbing, and diving. You're either braking hard or pedaling hard the whole way. Still, with only 1,200 feet of elevation gain, the Lake Chabot Loop is suitable for all kinds of riders. The challenge of a few hills is compensated by the sheer fun of the ride. This is a good place to gain some experience on a mountain bike.

You will have to put up with some irritating signs of civilization, though. In addition to the lake's busy marina and campground, you'll ride near a golf course and a shooting range. And if this is your first time here, you must pay careful attention to trail junctions. There are a ton of them. Too many, you may surmise.

An advantage to the prolific junctions is that Lake Chabot's trails can be customized according to your desires and abilities. The route described here combines the

© ANN MARIE BROWN

The popular bike trail around Lake Chabot is a mix of paved, fire, and single-track roads.

paved West and East Shore Trails with several dirt fire roads for a 13.3-mile round-trip. The two paved trails are surprisingly scenic; they skirt the lake's edge, sometimes rising up along its steep walls, sometimes tracing a line just a few feet from the water.

Following the loop below, East Shore Trail's pavement ends 1.8 miles beyond the marina. Mountain bikers continue onward, walking their bikes over a bridge to connect with Honker Bay Trail (some use Live Oak Trail to make their loop; I prefer Honker Bay because it stays along the lakeshore). Take a trail map with you (they're available for free at the trailhead) to negotiate the long stretch of Brandon Trail; it intersects annoyingly with what seems like a million other trails. Still, it offers some wide views of San Francisco Bay.

For more information, contact East Bay Regional Park District, 510/635-0135 or 510/562-7275, www.ebparks.org.

Options

Families with young children and skinny-tire riders will want to stick to the paved East and West Shore Trails for a nine-mile out-and-back. If you want to turn your bike ride into a day at the lake, Lake Chabot Marina (510/247-2526) has boats for rent, plus a small café that sells hot dogs and coffee. Lake Chabot is stocked with trout, bass, and catfish, and fishing prospects are quite good.

Driving Directions

From Oakland, drive east on I-580 and take the Dutton/Estudillo Avenue exit in San Leandro. Drive 0.5 mile, then turn left on Estudillo Avenue and drive 0.4 mile. Bear right at the Y with Lake Chabot Road and drive 2.5 miles to a T-junction. Turn left, then left again into Lake Chabot Marina.

Route Directions

0.0 Park at Lake Chabot Marina and head for the east side of the picnic area to the start of East Shore Trail. *Supplies are available at the marina store and café. A trail map is posted on a signboard next to the marina café.*

1.8 LEFT across narrow bridge at end of paved East Shore Trail; walk your bike.

1.9 LEFT on Honker Bay Trail.

3.5 Join paved campground road; ride through family campground on main road.

4.0 RIGHT on Towhee Trail.

4.8 LEFT on Brandon Trail (easy to miss—watch for it!).

4.9 Parking lot and restrooms; cross road and pick up Brandon Trail on other side.

5.5 LEFT on Logger's Loop Trail (or RIGHT to stay on Brandon Trail and save 0.9 mile).

6.6 Back on Brandon Trail.

8.4 LEFT and across stone bridge to LEFT on Jackson Grade to Goldenrod Trail.

8.8 Grass Valley Staging Area; stay on Goldenrod Trail.

10.2 RIGHT on Bass Cove Trail.

11.5 LEFT on paved West Shore Trail.

13.3 Arrive at starting point.

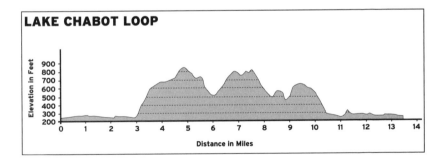

15 PALOMARES ROAD
east of Hayward and Fremont

PAVED ROAD WITH MINIMAL CAR TRAFFIC

Difficulty: 3   **Total Distance:** 20.2 miles

Riding Time: 1-2 hours   **Elevation Gain:** 1,900 feet

Summary: A fun training ride takes you on a winding road in the Sunol countryside, with the chance to stop for wine-tasting on weekends.

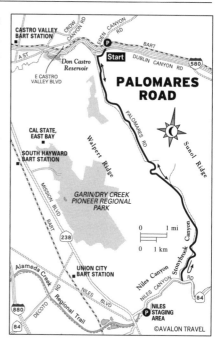

For a short stint in my life, I had the pleasure of living in the peaceful Sunol countryside, where on Sunday mornings I would awaken to the sounds of birds chirping and my roommate yelling, "Get up! Let's go ride Palomares Road."

And so we did, along with dozens of other East Bay cyclists, almost every Sunday, rain or shine. It was a happy habit that put some country into our urban lives.

The good news is that Palomares Road is still a peaceful country road, despite the fact that it's bordered by busy highways on both ends. The road is perfect for a quick 20-mile training ride after work or on the weekends. It's remote enough that it feels like a getaway even though it's remarkably close to home for riders in the southeast Bay Area.

Some cyclists make a loop out of Palomares Road by riding Dublin Canyon Road to the north and Niles Canyon Road (Highway 84) to the south, then using Foothill Road as the east connector. I don't recommend it. These three roads were viable for cyclists a decade or so ago, but are now heavily trafficked almost 24 hours a day. Besides, who wants to ride on a freeway frontage road after spinning though Palomares Road's lovely forested scenery?

Palomares Road ascends from both ends; the high point is almost exactly in the middle. That means you get an invigorating climb and a fun descent in both directions. In between, you have many rolling curves and a chance to ride as fast as 40 mph on the downhills, if you so choose.

Palomares Road is a peaceful country lane bordered by busy highways on both ends.

Options

If you're more into savoring your rides than speeding through them, note that two wineries are open on Palomares Road: Chouinard Winery (510/582-9900, www.chouinard.com) and Westover Vineyards (510/537-3932, www.westoverwinery.com). Both offer drop-in wine-tasting on weekends noon–5 P.M.

Driving Directions

From Hayward, drive four miles east on I-580 and take the Eden Canyon Road/Palomares Road exit. Turn left, cross under the freeway, and park on the north side of the freeway in the dirt pullout (start of Eden Canyon Road).

Route Directions

0.0 Park in the dirt pullout at the start of Eden Canyon Road, by the I-580 freeway overpass. Ride under the overpass and cross Dublin Canyon Road to access Palo Verde Road. *Supplies are available in Hayward or Dublin.*

0.4 LEFT on Palomares Road.

5.4 Summit of Palomares Road.

6.3 Chouinard Winery.

6.6 Westover Vineyards.

10.1 End of Palomares Road at Highway 84. TURN AROUND.

20.2 Arrive at starting point.

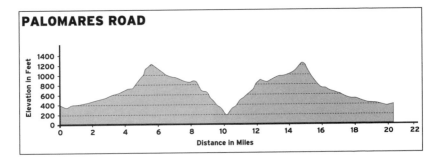

16 MORGAN TERRITORY ROAD
Livermore to Clayton

PAVED ROADS WITH MINIMAL CAR TRAFFIC

Difficulty: 4

Total Distance: 46.4 miles

Riding Time: 3-4 hours

Elevation Gain: 3,500 feet

Summary: If the hustle and bustle of the East Bay has started to wear you down, you need a ride on bucolic Morgan Territory Road.

One of the finest roads in the East Bay crosses through the Black Hills north of Livermore and passes by the eastern flank of mighty Mount Diablo and neighboring North Peak. Morgan Territory Road, as it is known, leaves the shopping centers and I-580 freeway traffic far behind as it carves a narrow path through hillside grasslands and scenic oak woodlands.

As an out-and-back ride, this route from Livermore to Clayton has a good hill climb in both directions, so a stop in Clayton for lunch is recommended, and also perhaps a rest stop near the road's summit at elevation 2,100 feet, near Morgan Territory Re-

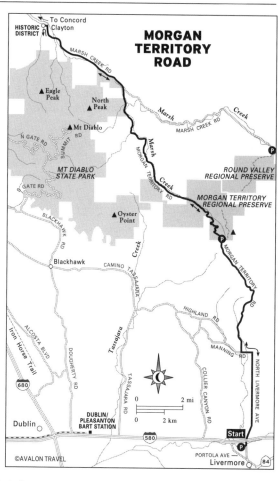

gional Preserve. (If traffic is heavy, you may want to ride this route in the opposite direction; see *Options*.) Your main concern is the weather—this kind of climbing in these sunny, exposed hills should be reserved for the cooler days of fall,

Morgan Territory Road

winter, and spring. Another concern is the narrowness of Morgan Territory Road; one car and one bike makes a crowd. Fortunately cars are few and far between.

Although it seems sensible to make a loop out of this ride by returning from Clayton to Livermore on Marsh Creek Road and Vasco Road, a five-mile stretch of Vasco Road has been widened in recent years, making it as fast and hectic as a freeway. Intrepid riders may still want to make this loop, but be forewarned of the long hill climb on Vasco Road with cars peeling by you at 70 mph. Although the road's shoulder is wide, riding it is just plain stressful. An out-and-back on Morgan Territory Road is safer, more scenic, and far more relaxing.

For more information on Morgan Territory Regional Preserve, contact East Bay Regional Park District, 510/635-0135 or 510/562-7275, www.ebparks.org.

Options

Note that depending on what day of the week and what hour of the day you ride, you could face a daunting amount of car traffic on Marsh Creek Road. If that's the case, it's best to do this ride in reverse, so you are heading east and downhill on Marsh Creek Road and can keep pace with the cars. There is very little shoulder on this stretch, so you'll need to be in the car lane, and you'll need to ride fast.

Driving Directions

From Livermore on I-580, take the North Livermore Avenue exit and park at the shopping center just south of I-580 on North Livermore Avenue.

Route Directions

0.0 Park at the shopping center just south of I-580 on North Livermore Avenue and ride north, crossing under the freeway. Set your odometer on the north side of I-580. *Supplies are available in Livermore.*

3.5 LEFT on Manning Road.

4.0 RIGHT on Morgan Territory Road.

4.7 Road narrows to single lane.

9.5 Entrance to Morgan Territory Regional Preserve on right. *Water is available.*

15.0 Road widens to two lanes.

18.7 LEFT on Marsh Creek Road.

22.7 LEFT on Marsh Creek Road (also called Clayton Road in Clayton).

23.2 Arrive in Clayton historic district. TURN AROUND. *Supplies are available in Clayton.*

46.2 Arrive at starting point.

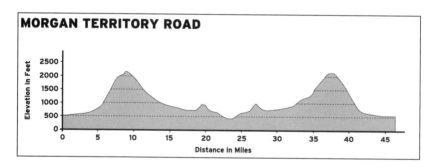

17 LIVERMORE WINERY RIDE
Livermore

PAVED ROADS WITH MODERATE CAR TRAFFIC

Difficulty: 2   **Total Distance:** 19.5 miles (or 24.5-mile option)

Riding Time: 2 hours   **Elevation Gain:** 800 feet

Summary: Nearly a dozen wineries await cyclists who choose to ramble through the Livermore countryside.

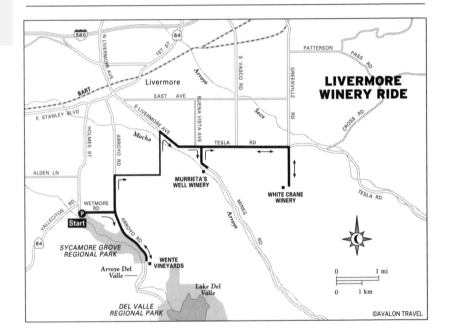

The town of Livermore, well known for being the home of Lawrence Livermore Laboratories and a huge collection of windmills, was founded in 1869 as a farming community. Cattle and sheep ranching and hay and grain production made the fertile area prosperous for more than a century. Even today the annual June rodeo is still the biggest show in town, although Livermore's agricultural legacy has largely shifted to vineyards and wine production. All the better for cyclists, who can ride this easy tour of rolling hills and stop to taste the products of nearly a dozen wineries.

While planning your ride, remember two things: First, if you want to do much wine-tasting, ride on Saturday or Sunday, because many smaller wineries are not open on weekdays. Second, consider the weather in Livermore. Pick a cool day and bring along a picnic for the ride's finale, when you return to shady Sycamore Grove Park (925/373-5770).

The route directions show only the mileage along the main roads from winery to winery. Each time you choose to stop at one of the wineries, your mileage will increase as you ride up and down its driveway. I'm assuming you won't stop to taste at every winery mentioned (if you did, your bike-handling skills would be severely compromised), so adjust your mileage according to your chosen stops. And if you want to shorten the ride, skip the out-and-back to Wente Vineyards on Arroyo Road (at 0.7 mile) and save 3.5 miles. Just go left on Arroyo Road instead.

If you can arrange it, try to get tickets in advance for one of the outdoor summer concerts at Wente Vineyards (5050 Arroyo Rd., 925/456-2300, www.wentevineyards.com). You can ride all afternoon, have dinner at a restaurant in town, and go to a show in the evening. Concerts are held June–September each year and feature well-known acts like Lyle Lovett and Chris Isaak.

Have fun. And don't forget to drink some water with that wine.

Options
If you feel like riding a bit more, Sycamore Grove Park has a 2.5-mile paved bike path through its grasslands and groves of sycamores. An out-and-back will add an easy, pleasant 5 miles to your day.

Driving Directions
From I-580 in Livermore, take the North Livermore Avenue exit and turn south. Drive 1 mile through downtown Livermore. Turn right on Stanley Boulevard (Highway 84), then left on Holmes Street. Follow Holmes Street for about 2 miles, then turn left on East Vallecitos Road (signed for the Veterans Hospital), which becomes Wetmore Road. Turn right into Sycamore Grove Park in 0.3 mile.

Route Directions
0.0 Park at Sycamore Grove Park, then ride out to Wetmore Road and turn RIGHT. *Supplies are available in Livermore and at several wineries along the route.*

0.3 Livermore Valley Cellars.

0.7 RIGHT on Arroyo Road.

2.5 Wente Vineyards, Golf Course, Restaurant, and Visitor Center. TURN AROUND.

4.2 STRAIGHT at junction of Wetmore and Arroyo Roads.

5.0 RIGHT on Marina Avenue. Watch for speed "humps" (not bumps!).

6.0 LEFT on Wente Street.

6.5 RIGHT on Concannon Boulevard.

6.9 RIGHT on South Livermore Avenue, which becomes Tesla Road.

7.6 Concannon Vineyard.

7.9 RIGHT on Mines Road.

8.2 Murrieta's Well Winery. TURN AROUND.

8.5 RIGHT on Tesla Road.

8.8 Steven Kent Winery.

8.9 Wente Estate Vineyards (different from Wente Vineyards).

9.6 Rios-Lovell Winery.

10.1 Cedar Mountain Winery.

10.5 Garre Vineyard and Café.

10.6 RIGHT on Greenville Road.

11.1 Poppy Ridge Golf Course.

11.6 Bent Creek Winery.

11.7 White Crane Vineyards. TURN AROUND.

13.0 LEFT on Tesla Road.

16.1 LEFT on Concannon Boulevard.

16.5 LEFT on Wente Street.

17.0 RIGHT on Marina Avenue.

18.0 LEFT on Arroyo Road.

18.8 RIGHT on Wetmore Road.

19.5 Arrive at starting point.

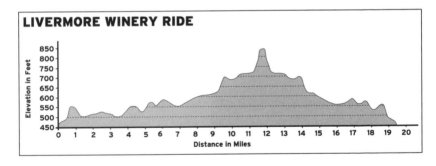

18 ALAMEDA CREEK TRAIL   BEST ◖

Fremont to Coyote Hills Regional Park

PAVED BIKE PATH

Difficulty: 1   **Total Distance:** 24 miles (or longer options)

Riding Time: 2 hours   **Elevation Gain:** 200 feet

Summary: Enjoy miles of car-free riding on a paved trail that parallels Alameda Creek from Fremont to the shores of San Francisco Bay.

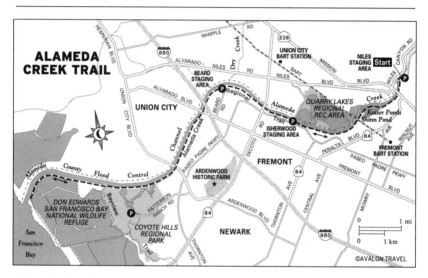

Alameda Creek, the largest stream in Alameda County, was once a valuable resource to the Ohlone Indians who settled along its banks. Today Alameda Creek Trail follows the creek from the mouth of Niles Canyon in Fremont 12 miles west to San Francisco Bay.

The trail is actually two parallel trails on the south and north banks of the creek. The south-side trail (paved) is for bikers, hikers, and runners, and the north side (unpaved) is for equestrians, too. The south-side trail, described here, accesses Coyote Hills Regional Park, where more riding is available.

Everything is in place here to make your ride easy. Unlike some trails in the East Bay's impressive system of paved recreation paths, the Alameda Creek Trail is unique in that it is uninterrupted by street intersections, so you have 12 miles of worry-free riding in both directions. Mileage markers are installed along the trail, and water and restrooms are available at several points. Even when the afternoon westerly wind comes up from the bay, it will be at your back for the slightly uphill ride home (provided you got an early start, of course).

Don't forget your binoculars for birdwatching when you ride on the Alameda Creek Trail to Coyote Hills Regional Park.

Alameda Creek Trail passes under highway overpasses and alongside neighborhood backyards, so it isn't exactly a nature trail, although you will probably spot a variety of birds along the narrow-channeled creek. Snowy egrets are often seen in abundance.

For more information, contact East Bay Regional Park District, 510/635-0135 or 510/562-7275, www.ebparks.org.

Options

If you're clamoring for something more, well, natural, add on a ride in Coyote Hills Regional Park, a bayside park with lots of wildlife and fascinating Native American history. Skinny-tire riders are restricted to adding 3.5 paved miles on the park's Bayview Trail, but mountain bikers can pedal around on the numerous dirt trails that roll up and down Coyote's rounded hills. Those who enjoy steep ups and fast downs should not miss the Red Hill Trail in particular. Another great option is to connect from the Alameda Creek Trail to Quarry Lakes Park (at Isherwood Way, the Sequoia Bridge, or the Niles Gate). This lovely park has its own small network of biking trails as well as fishing and swimming opportunities at Horseshoe Lake and Rainbow Lake.

Driving Directions

From I-680 in Fremont, take the Mission Boulevard exit and drive northwest for four miles to Highway 84/Niles Canyon Road. Turn right, then right again on Old Canyon Road. The staging area is on the left.

Route Directions

0.0 Park at Niles Staging Area and follow the trail out of the parking lot. *Water and restrooms are available at the staging area and along the trail.*

1.4 Pass Kaiser and Shinn Ponds.

2.6 Bridge at end of Thornton Avenue.

3.5 Isherwood Staging Area.

4.3 Decoto Road.

5.4 End of Beard Road; Beard Staging Area.

6.1 I-880.

6.4 Alvarado Boulevard.

7.8 Newark Boulevard.

9.7 Sign at base of hill leading to Coyote Hills Regional Park.

12.0 Edge of San Francisco Bay. TURN AROUND. *Or take the 50-foot connector trail from Alameda Creek Trail to the paved Bayview Trail in Coyote Hills Regional Park, adding on a 3.5-mile paved loop. Mountain bikers can add on several miles of dirt riding in the park.*

24.0 Arrive at starting point.

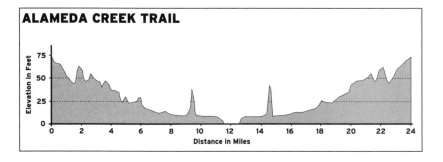

PENINSULA AND SOUTH BAY

© ANN MARIE BROWN

BEST BIKE RIDES

€ Families
Sawyer Camp Recreation Trail, **page 172**
Berry Creek Falls Bike and Hike, **page 225.**

€ High Overlooks
Montara Mountain, **page 169.**
Mount Hamilton, **page 216.**

€ Single-Track Rides
El Corte de Madera Creek Loop, **page 180.**
Saratoga Gap Loop, **page 207.**
Middle Ridge Loop, **page 222.**

€ Waterfront Rides
Pescadero and San Gregorio Loop, **page 197.**

€ Wildlife-Viewing
Sawyer Camp Recreation Trail, **page 172.**

Spend a Saturday afternoon in the highlands of

Skyline Ridge or the Santa Cruz Mountains, and you'll be convinced that mountain biking is the most popular recreational sport in the South Bay. But pass that same afternoon in the Peninsula town of Woodside or on the hilly roads of Saratoga or Mount Hamilton, and you'll quickly change your tune. In these South Bay locales, road biking is the sport of choice, most often partaken on ultra-pricey machines with titanium or carbon frames and the highest-tech components. The reality is that there is plentiful pedaling for all types of riders in this region south of San Francisco.

Those seeking dirt trails will find them in abundance in several state parks – Big Basin Redwoods, McNee Ranch, Portola Redwoods, Henry W. Coe – as well as in a patchwork of lands on the northern Peninsula that are managed by the Golden Gate National Recreation Area. A few county parks also open their trails to mountain bikers, including the lush redwood groves of Pescadero Creek and the oak-studded grasslands of Joseph D. Grant on the lower slopes of Mount Hamilton near San Jose.

But perhaps the biggest bonanza for fat-tire lovers is the wealth of preserves that are managed by the Midpeninsula Regional Open Space District, most of which border Skyline Boulevard (Highway 35), running across the spine of the northern Santa Cruz Mountains. Here, more than three dozen trailheads are found within a 50-mile stretch of road, providing access to more than 100 miles of bike-friendly trails (an additional 200 trail miles are open only to hikers and equestrians). On the ocean side of Skyline Ridge, dense groves of redwoods and Douglas firs soak up the coastal fog, whereas the bay side is a mosaic of grasslands interspersed by oak and bay woodlands. Deer, coyotes, and bobcats are commonly seen in this ridgetop-hugging land. Some of the best wildflower-viewing in the entire Bay Area is possible in several of the open space district's preserves, most noticeably Russian Ridge and Long Ridge.

Road cyclists, too, flock to the Skyline Boulevard region, but usually only while passing through on long, demanding tours from the Peninsula towns to the coast. Far from traffic-clogged U.S. 101 lie meandering country roads and old stagecoach routes that travel the more rural regions of San Mateo County. The historic coastal villages of Pescadero and San Gregorio have long been favorite stopping points for high-mileage road riders — especially those seeking shelter from the frequent coastal winds.

Less ambitious bicyclists, including those pulling Burley trailers or sporting training wheels, also have South Bay trails that suit their needs. The Sawyer Camp Recreation Trail, which runs alongside the scenic shoreline of Crystal Springs Reservoir, is one of the most popular paved bike trails in the entire Bay Area. It's a great place for a quick after-work workout or a casual Sunday family cruise. Those looking for a longer recreational ride can head south to San Jose's Coyote Creek Trail, where you can pedal nearly 30 miles on a smooth paved trail that is completely free of car traffic, or even take a turn around the velodrome at Coyote Hellyer County Park.

The South Bay may go down in history as the focal point of the dot-com boom and bust, but those who ride here know it better for its rolling inland hills, rugged coastline, towering redwood forests, miles of ranch and farming lands, and soothing wealth of open spaces. Whether you choose to ride on the South Bay's roads or trails, you'll be witness to an urban wilderness like no other.

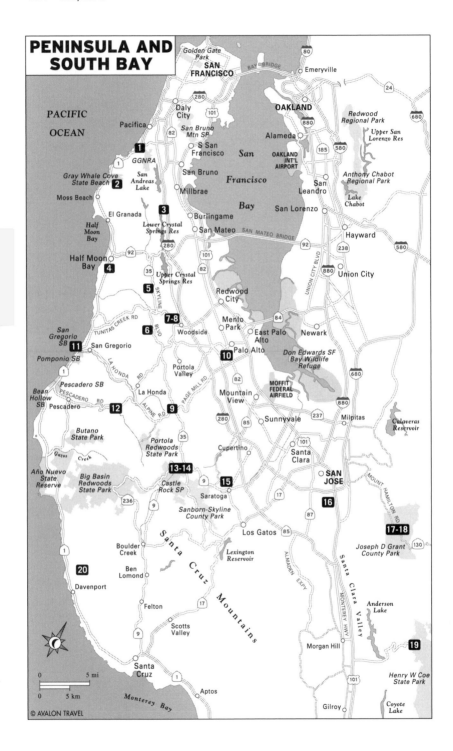

PENINSULA AND SOUTH BAY

TRAIL NAME	LEVEL	DISTANCE	TIME	ELEVATION	PAGE
1 Sweeney Ridge Loop	3	7.3 mi	2 hr	1,100 ft	166
2 Montara Mountain	3	9.6 mi	2 hr	2,000 ft	169
3 Sawyer Camp Recreation Trail	1	12 mi	1 hr	250 ft	172
4 Half Moon Bay Back Roads	3	24.1 mi	2 hr	1,500 ft	175
5 Purisima Redwoods Loop	3	10 mi	2-3 hr	1,600 ft	177
6 El Corte de Madera Creek Loop	3	10.5 mi	2 hr	1,400 ft	180
7 Woodside to Skyline Short Loop	4	20 mi	1.5-2 hr	2,200 ft	184
8 Woodside to Coast Long Loop	5	57.1 mi	5-7 hr	5,800 ft	187
9 Russian Ridge and Coal Creek Loop	2	7.3 mi	1.5 hr	800 ft	191
10 Stanford and Portola Valley Loop	2	18 mi	1.5 hr	750 ft	194
11 Pescadero and San Gregorio Loop	3	28.7 mi	2 hr	1,200 ft	197
12 Old Haul Road Loop	3	17.6 mi	3 hr	2,100 ft	200
13 Big Basin and Boulder Creek Loop	4	43 mi	3-4 hr	3,300 ft	203
14 Saratoga Gap Loop	3	12.9 mi	2-3 hr	1,600 ft	207
15 Monte Bello Loop	4	27 mi	3 hr	2,300 ft	210
16 Coyote Creek Trail	2	29.4 mi	2-3 hr	400 ft	213
17 Mount Hamilton	4	23 mi	2 hr	2,700 ft	216
18 Grant Ranch Loop	3	10.9 or 12 mi	2 hr	1,600 ft	219
19 Middle Ridge Loop	4	10.8 mi	2 hr	2,100 ft	222
20 Berry Creek Falls Bike and Hike	2	11.6 mi	2.5 hr	550 ft	225

∎ SWEENEY RIDGE LOOP

Golden Gate National Recreation Area near Pacifica

DIRT ROAD AND PAVED ROADS WITH MODERATE CAR TRAFFIC

Difficulty: 3   **Total Distance:** 7.3 miles

Riding Time: 2 hours   **Elevation Gain:** 1,100 feet

Summary: This mostly dirt loop delivers sweeping ocean views − on rare clear days − and the chance to visit the San Francisco Bay Discovery Site.

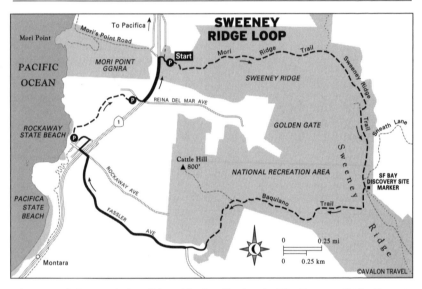

It's steep, it's fast, and it's well loved by Pacifica locals. The Sweeney Ridge Loop is the perfect length for a good bout of exercise, and it can be completed in a couple of hours. Better still, on clear days it offers one of the best views in the Bay Area, an incredible 360-degree panorama from the top of Sweeney Ridge. This vista takes in the Pacific coastline and San Francisco Bay as well as the landmass to the east, north, and south—including Montara Mountain, Mount Tamalpais, Mount Diablo, Mount Hamilton, Point Reyes, Point San Pedro, and the Farallon Islands. But remember, clear days are rare in Pacifica, especially in summer. If you want to see the view, ride here in one of the other seasons.

This loop route isn't for the aerobically challenged. It starts out with a serious climb on Mori Ridge Trail, an old dirt road, gaining 700 feet in 1.3 miles. Don't expect a warm-up; you just get into your lowest gear at the trailhead and crank uphill. The trail leads through open grasslands and coastal scrub, with occasional Monterey pines presenting a chance for shade. When Mori Ridge Trail meets up with Sweeney Ridge Trail, the heart-pumping work is over. Turn right for a much easier cruise to an old Nike missile site, then follow the paved trail south from the decaying military buildings to the San Francisco Bay Discovery Site. It was here, at the 1,220-foot summit on top of Sweeney Ridge, that Gaspar de Portolá first sighted San Francisco Bay on November 4, 1769. A stone monument commemorates the discovery.

You're back on dirt now and ready to start your descent on Baquiano Trail. The trail gets steeper and faster as it goes, so watch your speed. Remember: Hikers and dog walkers also use this trail, and they don't appreciate getting run over by bikes. You'll drop down to a gate at the end of Fassler Avenue in Pacifica, then continue steeply downhill to Highway 1, now on pavement and in the company of car traffic. Cross to the west side of the highway at Rockaway Beach Avenue, pick up the short but scenic bike path alongside Calera Creek, then cross Highway 1 again at Reina del Mar Avenue. The last stretch back to your car is, unfortunately, the least pleasant of the trip: a 0.3-mile stretch on the wide Highway 1 shoulder, then a steep 0.3-mile stint up the driveway to Shell Dance Nursery and back to the trailhead. But the rest of the loop makes it worth it.

For more information, contact the Golden Gate National Recreation Area Presidio Visitor Center, 415/561-4323, www.nps.gov/goga; or the Pacifica Visitor Center and Chamber of Commerce, 650/355-4122, www.pacificachamber.com.

Options

Bicyclists who would like to visit the San Francisco Bay Discovery Site and old Nike missile site without working so hard to do so can begin their ride at the Sneath Lane trailhead in San Bruno. From I-280, take the Sneath Lane/San Bruno Avenue exit and head west. Drive 1.9 miles on Sneath Lane to the trailhead parking area. The paved Sweeney Ridge Trail begins here and climbs a moderate 2.2 miles to the top of the ridge.

Driving Directions

From Highway 1 in Pacifica, turn east into the driveway for Shell Dance Nursery (north of Reina del Mar Avenue and south of Sharp Park Road). Drive 0.3 mile, past the nursery buildings, to the signed Sweeney Ridge trailhead parking area. (If you are driving south on Highway 1, you will have to make a U-turn and head north to enter the Shell Dance Nursery driveway.)

Route Directions

0.0 Park at the Sweeney Ridge trailhead by Shell Dance Nursery. Begin riding on the trail heading uphill from the trailhead sign. *Supplies are available in Pacifica.*

1.3 RIGHT at junction of Mori Ridge Trail and Sweeney Ridge Trail.

2.1 Nike missile site; dirt trail meets up with paved trail along the ridgetop; follow paved trail.

2.6 STRAIGHT on dirt trail where pavement turns sharply left.

2.7 RIGHT on Baquiano Trail at San Francisco Bay Discovery Site marker.

4.0 Go through gate.

4.1 LEFT at trail fork.

4.4 Pass water tank; trail becomes old paved road.

4.5 Go through gate at end of Fassler Avenue; watch for cars on downhill.

5.8 Cross Highway 1 to Rockaway Beach Avenue.

5.9 RIGHT on Dondee Way.

6.0 LEFT on San Marlo Way.

6.1 Parking lot by beach; pick up paved bike trail on right side of parking lot.

6.6 Bike trail meets the parking lot by Reina del Mar Avenue; ride out to Highway 1 and cross to its east side (don't stay on the bike trail, which travels on the west side of Highway 1).

6.7 LEFT on Highway 1; ride north using wide shoulder, passing police station.

7.0 RIGHT at Shell Dance Nursery driveway; steep uphill.

7.3 Arrive at starting point.

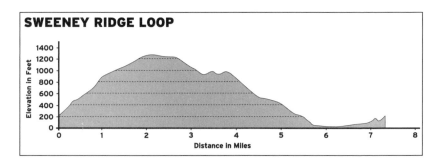

2 MONTARA MOUNTAIN

BEST **C**

McNee Ranch State Park, north of Half Moon Bay

DIRT ROAD AND DETERIORATING PAVEMENT

Difficulty: 3   **Total Distance:** 9.6 miles

Riding Time: 2 hours   **Elevation Gain:** 2,000 feet

Summary: Each time you pause to catch your breath on this coastal summit ride, sublime ocean vistas await.

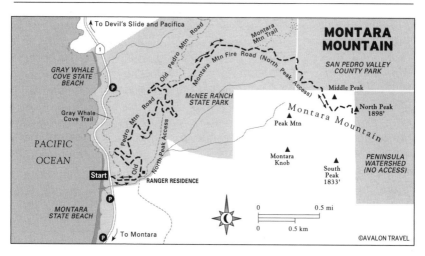

You like a long, sustained hill climb and a lightning-fast descent? You get them both on this ride from the Pacific Ocean to the top of Montara Mountain, elevation 1,898 feet. Make sure your body has plenty of fuel and water for the 4.8-mile climb up, and wear your sturdiest helmet for the ride down.

Aside from the heart- and leg-pumping work, there isn't much to think about on this ride, which has almost no intersections. Instead, you can focus on the views, which are downright spectacular on clear days. You ride with the ocean mostly at your back for the first 1.5 miles, heading deep into Montara Mountain's coastal canyon. Gradually the trail rises above the valleys and starts to show off glimpses of the blue Pacific. At the 2.2-mile mark, where two posts mark a side trail off-limits to bikes, the panorama opens wide, exposing the crashing surf and tall cliffs of Montara State Beach and Gray Whale Cove.

Here you can pause to consider how often the section of Highway 1 below you—aptly named Devil's Slide—has been closed due to landslides, effectively sealing off the people of Montara and nearby communities from most of the rest of the world and creating traffic nightmares on Highway 92, the only other nearby

This view of the treacherous stretch of coast known as Devil's Slide is a good reason for a rest stop on the ascent up Montara Mountain.

access to the coast from the Peninsula. The most recent long-term closure was in 2006, when the road was closed April–August. Residents of the coast will continue to hold their breath until late 2012 or early 2013, when two tunnels through the base of Montara Mountain should be completed, which will completely eliminate this accident-prone stretch of Highway 1. At that time, the old highway and the land around it is scheduled to be made available for public recreation, which should give bikers even more to cheer about.

The views keep expanding as you pedal onward and upward. When at last you attain Montara Mountain's transmitter tower–littered summit, your view expands to include the north and east: Mount Tamalpais, the skyline of San Francisco, the famous sign on U.S. 101 proclaiming South San Francisco the Industrial City, San Mateo Bridge, San Francisco Bay, plus Mount Diablo in the background. This is one of the most all-encompassing views possible in the Bay Area.

The trail's grade is fairly moderate all the way up except for one 0.5-mile stretch at 2.6 miles, which is *really* steep (it gains 500 feet in 0.5 mile). Making matters worse, this stretch is also often extremely rutted. The path's first 2.4 miles are a mix of deteriorating pavement, gravel, and dirt (often squeezed into single-track by encroaching pampas grass). You're riding on old San Pedro Mountain Road, which used to be the route from Montara to Pacifica before precarious Highway 1 was built. The last 2.4 miles follow Montara Mountain Fire Road, a wide dirt road. Because of its rough surface, descending can be like riding on ball bearings;

it's difficult to control your speed. Move your butt way back off your seat or you'll go down for sure. Guess how I know?

For more information, contact Montara State Beach or McNee Ranch State Park, 650/726-8819 or 650/726-8820.

Driving Directions

From Half Moon Bay, drive north on Highway 1 for 10 miles to just north of Montara State Beach and La Costanera Restaurant and just south of Devil's Slide. The trailhead is marked by a yellow metal gate on the east side of the highway, with parking for about six cars. If this lot is full, park 0.2 mile farther south at Montara State Beach.

Route Directions

0.0 Park at McNee Ranch trailhead by the yellow metal gate. Begin riding on the wide road behind the gate (not the single-track trail). *Supplies are available in Montara, one mile south.*

0.2 LEFT at fork by ranger's house.

1.7 Dirt road merges in from the right.

2.2 Coastal viewpoint where hiker's trail leads west (signed as No Bikes).

2.4 RIGHT on dirt Montara Mountain Fire Road (deteriorating pavement veers to the left); prepare for brutal 0.5-mile climb.

3.5 Pass Montara Mountain Trail on left (hikers-only trail from San Pedro Valley County Park).

4.4 South Peak of Montara Mountain on left; continue straight.

4.8 Arrive at North Peak of Montara Mountain. TURN AROUND. *Climb up the rocky, short trail (about 20 feet) next to the communication towers for the best view of the day.*

9.6 Arrive at starting point.

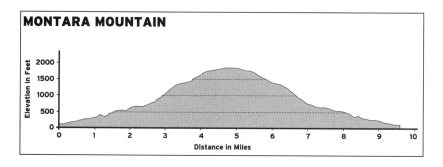

3 SAWYER CAMP RECREATION TRAIL

BEST ◖

Crystal Springs Reservoir near Hillsborough and Millbrae

PAVED BIKE PATH

Difficulty: 1   **Total Distance:** 12 miles

Riding Time: 1 hour   **Elevation Gain:** 250 feet

Summary: A paved trail skirts the edge of Lower Crystal Springs Reservoir, offering easy pedaling and a good chance for wildlife sightings.

Few bike trails are as well loved and well used as the Sawyer Camp Trail. This paved, car-free recreation trail is long enough so you can feel like you got some exercise riding it, easy enough so that even the most casual rider can try it, and surprisingly scenic as well. Its only drawback is its popularity: With so many people living nearby on the northern Peninsula, the trail is almost always packed with walkers, runners, in-line skaters, and baby strollers, in addition to bikers. No matter; just get here early to avoid the crowds, especially on weekends.

The trail travels the length of Lower Crystal Springs Reservoir, then leads through marshlands to southern San Andreas Lake, ending just beyond the lake's dam at Hillcrest Boulevard in Millbrae. Unlike many paved recreation trails, it isn't as straight as a stick; it twists and curves gracefully around the reservoir's shoreline. You have a good chance of seeing deer, raptors, herons, and egrets somewhere along the route.

The ride is an easy cruise; you probably won't even shift gears for the first 4.5 miles. The only noticeable hill is in the last stretch near San Andreas Lake's dam. Be sure to make a stop to see the Jepson laurel tree, 3.5 miles in and 25 feet off the trail (near a picnic area). More than 600 years old and 55 feet tall, the tree is the oldest and largest living California laurel, named for botanist Willis Jepson.

Another of the trail's highlights is a plaque on a boulder at trail's end at Hillcrest

Cyclists share the six-mile Sawyer Camp Recreation Trail with joggers and other users.

Boulevard, which marks the spot where Captain Gaspar de Portolá made camp after his discovery of San Francisco Bay in 1769.

Options

Mountain bikers don't have to stop at the Sawyer Camp Trail's end at Hillcrest Boulevard; a dirt trail continues from there to Larkspur Drive, where the paved San Andreas Trail begins and runs alongside the western half of San Andreas Lake. Road and mountain bikers looking for more mileage can connect the Sawyer Camp Trail with a ride on Cañada Road, two miles south of the Sawyer Camp Trailhead, which is good for riding any time but especially good every Sunday, when four miles of its length are closed to cars. For more information on Cañada Road Bicycle Sunday, contact San Mateo County Parks and Recreation, 650/363-4020, www.eparks.net.

Driving Directions

From I-280 in San Mateo, take the Highway 92 exit west, then turn right (north) immediately on Highway 35. Drive 0.5 mile to Crystal Springs Road and the trail entrance.

Route Directions

0.0 Park in the small parking lot by the trailhead, or alongside the road. Ride through the signed gate to enter the trail. *Water is available along the trail.*

3.5 Restrooms, drinking water, and picnic area by short path to Jepson laurel tree.

4.8 Beginning of hill climb.

5.1 Cross dam over San Andreas Lake.

6.0 Arrive at gate at Hillcrest Boulevard. TURN AROUND. *Note historic marker for Gaspar de Portolá's camp just past the gate.*

12.0 Arrive at starting point.

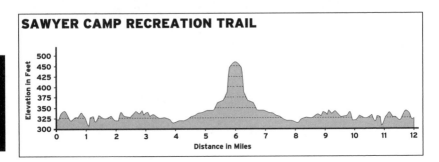

SAWYER CAMP RECREATION TRAIL

4 HALF MOON BAY BACK ROADS

south of Half Moon Bay

PAVED ROADS WITH MINIMAL CAR TRAFFIC

Difficulty: 3   **Total Distance:** 24.1 miles

Riding Time: 2 hours   **Elevation Gain:** 1,500 feet

Summary: Forget the crowds at the annual Pumpkin Festival – this road ride will show you the real Half Moon Bay.

Many Bay Area residents complain that the coastal resort town of Half Moon Bay has left its country roots behind and become too much of a city. This loop ride on Half Moon Bay's back roads (with a mere 6.8-mile stretch on busy Highway 1) proves that there's still plenty of country left in this coastal town; you just have to know where to find it.

The ride begins at the Half Moon Bay firehouse at the junction of Main Street and Higgins Canyon Road. The toughest part is the first 100 yards, in which you must use impeccable judgment when crossing the stream of cars on Highway 1. With this accomplished, you face a quick, level jaunt south on the highway, followed by another careful crossing and a left turn on Tunitas Creek Road. Now you're in the country, and you'll face nothing but quiet roads and pastoral scenery for the rest of your ride.

The only serious hill appears at mile

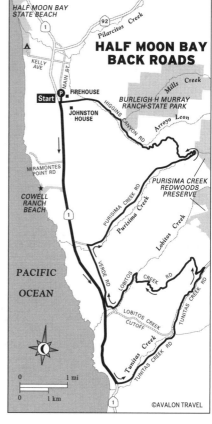

19.8, when Purisima Creek Road becomes Higgins Canyon Road at a hairpin turn in the road. Here you'll gain 400 feet in about two miles, then lose it again on your way back into town. Otherwise, there's a bit of climbing on Lobitos Creek Road, but it's nothing to complain about. The views of the remote coastal canyons will more than compensate.

Driving Directions

From Half Moon Bay at the junction of Highway 92 and Highway 1, head south on Highway 1 for 1.2 miles to Higgins Purisima Road (by the firehouse). Turn left and park along Main Street near the firehouse.

Route Directions

0.0 Park on the south end of Main Street in Half Moon Bay, near its junction with Higgins Canyon Road and Highway 1. Ride out the last few yards of Higgins Canyon Road and cross Highway 1 to head south. *Supplies are available on Main Street or Highway 1 in Half Moon Bay.*

1.9 Pass Cowell Ranch Beach turnoff.

6.8 LEFT on Tunitas Creek Road.

8.8 RIGHT at junction with Lobitos Creek Cutoff.

9.8 Enter redwoods.

10.4 LEFT on Lobitos Creek Road (a very sharp left turn).

14.6 RIGHT on Verde Road (parallels Highway 1 with nice views of the ocean).

16.2 RIGHT on Purisima Creek Road.

19.8 Pass entrance to Purisima Creek Redwoods Open Space Preserve at hairpin turn; road changes names to Higgins Purisima Road.

24.1 Arrive at starting point.

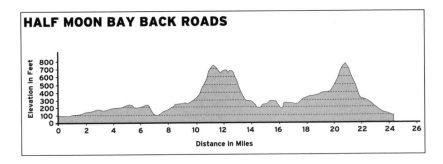

HALF MOON BAY BACK ROADS

5 PURISIMA REDWOODS LOOP

off Skyline Boulevard near Woodside

DIRT ROAD AND SINGLE-TRACK; PAVED ROAD WITH MODERATE CAR TRAFFIC

Difficulty: 3   **Total Distance:** 10 miles

Riding Time: 2-3 hours   **Elevation Gain:** 1,600 feet

Summary: Enjoy a redwood fantasy ride just a few miles south of San Francisco.

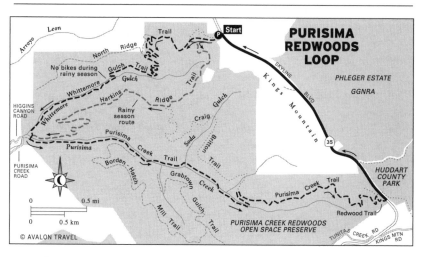

It might seem more sensible to start this loop ride from its lowest point, at the Purisima trailhead south of Half Moon Bay, so that you could climb uphill when you're fresh and save the downhill for the way home. But there's room for only a few cars at the Half Moon Bay trailhead, and these spaces are almost always filled. Unless you live in or near Half Moon Bay, it's not worth the drive to the trailhead only to discover there is no place to park.

Instead, start this ride at the top of the loop, at the large Purisima parking lot on Skyline Boulevard near Woodside. Folks who live in San Francisco and the northern Peninsula will find that this trailhead is close enough that they can show up after work on the long days of summer and still have enough daylight to complete the ride.

Summer is a key word here, because the Whittemore Gulch section of this trail is closed to bikes during the rainy season. It's a beautiful single-track trail tunneling through a flower-filled Douglas fir forest, with lots of fun twists and tight turns. (You access it 0.8 mile from the trailhead, after a rather bumpy ride on North Ridge Trail, a dirt road.)

The upper section of Whittemore Gulch Trail provides long-distance views of the Half Moon Bay coast, or Half Moon Bay fog, depending on the weather. The trail keeps descending until, at about two miles from the start, you enter a deep, dark redwood canyon. The area was logged in the late 1800s, so these are second- and third-growth trees, but impressive nonetheless. The return leg of the loop is uphill on Purisima Creek Trail, a gradual but steady climb alongside a pretty stream and some very large redwoods, followed by a quick, two-mile stint on paved Skyline Boulevard.

The single-track Whittemore Gulch Trail is a favorite route of mountain bikers in Purisima Creek Redwoods Open Space Preserve.

Options

If you must ride in the wet season, you can follow an alternate route in Purisima from the same trailhead: downhill on Harkins Ridge Trail and uphill on Purisima Creek Trail. The Midpeninsula Regional Open Space District (650/691-1200, www.openspace.org) keeps these wide trails open no matter what the weather. There's no comparison, though; Whittemore Gulch is the trail to ride in this park.

Driving Directions

From San Francisco, drive south on I-280 for 19 miles to the Highway 92 west exit. Go west on Highway 92 for 2.7 miles, then turn left (south) on Highway 35 (Skyline Boulevard). Drive 4.3 miles to the Purisima Creek Redwoods Open Space Preserve parking area on the right.

Route Directions

0.0 Park at Purisima Preserve parking lot on Skyline Boulevard. Follow North Ridge Trail (dirt road) from the parking lot (not the hikers-only trail). *Supplies are available eight miles south on Skyline Boulevard at Skylonda.*

0.3 Straight at junction with Harkins Ridge Trail.

0.8 LEFT on Whittemore Gulch Trail.

1.4 LEFT to stay on Whittemore Gulch Trail.

2.8 Cross footbridge; trail widens and levels out.

3.7 STRAIGHT at junction with Harkins Ridge Trail. Cross wide bridge ahead.

3.8 LEFT on Purisima Creek Trail on far side of bridge.

4.8 STRAIGHT at junction with Borden Hatch Mill Trail.

5.1 STRAIGHT at junction with Grabtown Gulch Trail.

6.1 RIGHT at junction with Soda Gulch/Craig Britton Trail.

7.8 RIGHT on Redwood Trail.

8.0 LEFT on Skyline Boulevard.

10.0 Arrive at starting point.

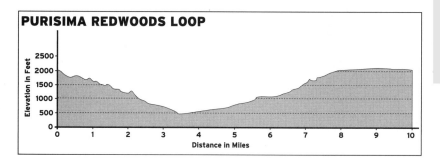

PURISIMA REDWOODS LOOP

6 EL CORTE DE MADERA CREEK LOOP

BEST **☾**

off Skyline Boulevard near Woodside

DIRT ROAD AND SINGLE-TRACK

Difficulty: 3

Total Distance: 10.5 miles

Riding Time: 2 hours

Elevation Gain: 1,400 feet

Summary: Miles of single-track trails await among the second- and third-growth redwoods in El Corte de Madera Creek canyon.

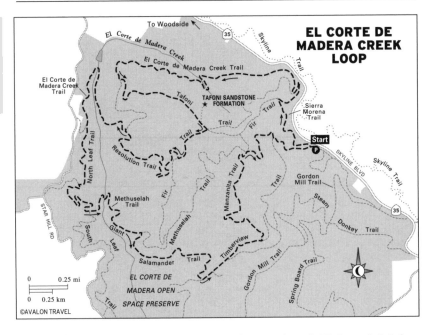

Of all the beautiful open-space lands on Skyline Boulevard, El Corte de Madera Creek Open Space Preserve is the one most favored by mountain bikers. Partly it's because almost every trail is open to bikes, and partly it's because so many of those trails are single-track. To sweeten the pot, the trail is densely shaded with second- and third-growth redwoods, making it a good choice for warm summer days when you want to ride where you won't bake in the sun.

The loop described below is designed to string together an abundance of single-track, but that means you have to put up with a lot of trail directions. One thing this preserve has plenty of, besides redwood trees, is junctions. It's common to see riders stopped at intersections here—they're usually consulting a map, or each other.

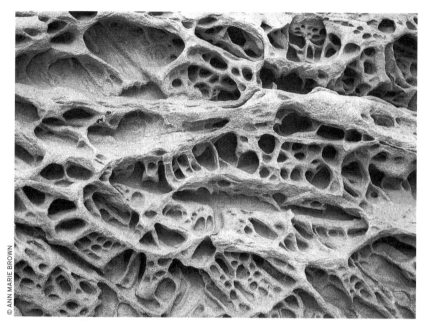

© ANN MARIE BROWN

honeycomb patterns in tafoni sandstone

This route is also designed to keep you away from the many hikers who walk the short trail to the preserve's main attraction, a tafoni sandstone formation. Except for a brief stretch where your paths may intersect, you should be far from the vast majority of pedestrians on this loop. Don't forget to bring a bike lock so you can chain up your wheels and walk the short path to see this cluster of 50-foot-high sandstone outcrops. Tafoni is a type of sandstone that is formed by years of weathering. The "glue" that holds the sandstone's individual sand grains together slowly erodes away, leaving honeycomb patterned, lace-like crevices and holes in the smooth rock. From an observation deck at the end of this 0.2-mile trail, you have a good vantage point for gazing in awe at the tafoni. Just don't think about riding your bike on this trail; it's for hiking only.

Another attraction this loop visits is the Old Growth Redwood, the only one left standing in this preserve. The tree is noticeably larger than its hundreds of second- and third-growth compatriots at El Corte de Madera Creek.

But mostly it's the riding you'll enjoy here. Highlights include the too-short romps on Giant Salamander and North Leaf Trails and a challenging climb on Resolution Trail (all single-track). Note that many of the trails are quite steep (even the single-tracks), so if you don't enjoy a lot of ups and downs, you won't be happy here. Overall, this is not a place for beginners to ride because of technical challenges, but intermediates will have a great time on the frequent sharp corners, steep ascents and descents, tree roots, and rocky and loose trail surfaces.

One more caveat: This preserve is subject to seasonal trail closures. During the rainy season, Leaf Trail, Methuselah Trail, Giant Salamander Trail, and a few others are often closed, and if so you'll have to limit your fun to the dry season from May to October.

For more information, contact the Midpeninsula Regional Open Space District, 650/691-1200, www.openspace.org.

Driving Directions

From San Francisco, drive south on I-280 for 19 miles to the Highway 92 west exit. Go west on Highway 92 for 2.7 miles, then turn left (south) on Highway 35 (Skyline Boulevard). Drive 8.9 miles to the trailhead parking on the west side of the road, 0.4 mile south of Skeggs Vista Point. (If this small lot is full, park at the vista point lot and ride south to this trailhead.)

Route Directions

0.0 Park at the CM02 gate and ride to your right (north) on Sierra Morena Trail. *Supplies are available in Skylonda, 3.4 miles south on Skyline Boulevard.*

0.6 RIGHT on Fir Trail.

0.8 Gate at Skyline Boulevard; turn sharply LEFT on Tafoni Trail.

0.9 RIGHT on El Corte de Madera Creek Trail.

1.6 LEFT to stay on El Corte de Madera Creek Trail (turns to single-track).

2.4 LEFT on Tafoni Trail.

3.2 Hiker's trail to tafoni sandstone formation on left. *Lock up your bike and walk the 0.2-mile trail to the see the tafoni.*

3.3 RIGHT (sharp) on Fir Trail at four-way junction.

3.5 LEFT at Vista Point Trail to stay on Fir Trail.

3.6 RIGHT on Resolution Trail (single-track).

4.7 LEFT on El Corte de Madera Creek Trail.

5.2 Cross El Corte de Madera Creek.

5.6 LEFT on North Leaf Trail (single-track).

6.7 LEFT on Methuselah Trail (single-track).

6.8 Cross El Corte de Madera Creek.

7.1 RIGHT on Giant Salamander Trail (single-track).

8.0 LEFT on Timberview Trail.

8.1 Old Growth Redwood. *Pay homage to the big tree.*

8.6 LEFT on Manzanita Trail (single-track).

9.7 RIGHT on Methuselah Trail at four-way junction.

10.1 LEFT to stay on Methuselah Trail.

10.5 Arrive at starting point.

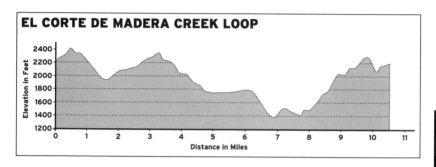

EL CORTE DE MADERA CREEK LOOP

7 WOODSIDE TO SKYLINE SHORT LOOP
Woodside to Skylonda

PAVED ROADS WITH MODERATE CAR TRAFFIC

Difficulty: 4   **Total Distance:** 20 miles

Riding Time: 1.5-2 hours   **Elevation Gain:** 2,200 feet

Summary: The bike-obsessed town of Woodside is the start of this popular 20-mile training loop.

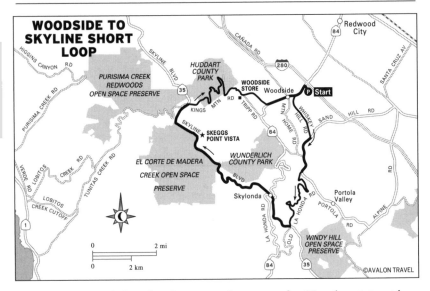

The Woodside to Skyline Short Loop is as close to a perfect 20-mile training ride as you can get. It supplies a killer 3.4-mile hill (Old La Honda Road from Woodside to Skyline Boulevard) and just enough mileage to keep your heart rate up for an hour or two. Yet it's remarkably scenic, provides convenient places to stop for fuel or rest, and offers a mix of wide bike lanes and less-traveled country roads. You'll have to put up with some traffic on Skyline Boulevard, but the payoff is worth it.

First, know that the tony community of Woodside is Bike Central. There isn't a more bike-friendly town anywhere in the Bay Area, a region filled with bike-friendly towns. And there isn't a more likely place to spot the most expensive bikes, the hottest gear, and the tautest leg muscles. It seems that people who can afford to live in Woodside have plenty of time for recreation and fitness. Try not to hold it against them.

Whiskey Hill and Sand Hill Roads both have wide bike lanes that will get you through the busy Woodside corridor. Then you begin your epic climb on

The historic Woodside Store (now a museum) is filled with local history.

extremely narrow Old La Honda Road, a former logging toll road that today twists and turns through second- and third-growth redwoods. On any weekend day you'll find members of local cycling clubs racing each other up this one-lane hill. Fortunately few car drivers use Old La Honda Road except for those who live on it. It's so steep and narrow that at its high terminus on Skyline Boulevard, it is signed "Downhill Bicycling Not Recommended."

The climb continues, more gradually now and with one 400-foot dip, as you cruise north on Skyline Boulevard. You can stop in Skylonda for a cool drink, or just continue onward to your big descent on Kings Mountain Road. Then it's back to Woodside, passing Huddart Park and the historic Woodside Store along the way. Stop in if it's open; the old store is now a museum with fascinating artifacts from the area's pioneer past.

Options

For more mileage and hills in the Woodside area, see ride 8, *Woodside to Coast Long Loop.*

Driving Directions

From I-280, take the Highway 84/Woodside exit and drive west for less than 0.25 mile to the Park and Ride lot.

Route Directions

0.0 Park at the Woodside Park and Ride lot. Ride west on Woodside Road (Highway 84). *Supplies are available in Woodside.*

0.5 LEFT on Whiskey Hill Road.

1.8 RIGHT on Sand Hill Road at Y-junction.

3.2 RIGHT on Old La Honda Road.

6.6 RIGHT on Skyline Boulevard.

8.1 Skylonda market and Alice's Restaurant at junction of Skyline and Highway 84. *Supplies are available.*

11.9 Skeggs Vista Point on right.

13.6 RIGHT on Kings Mountain Road.

16.5 Entrance to Huddart Park on left. *Water is available.*

17.7 LEFT at stop sign at Entrance Way.

17.9 Historic Woodside Store at Tripp Road junction. *Stop in to the museum to see the local history exhibits.*

18.6 LEFT on Woodside Road (Highway 84).

19.4 Downtown Woodside. *Supplies are available.*

19.5 STRAIGHT at junction with Whiskey Hill Road (start of loop).

20.0 Arrive at starting point.

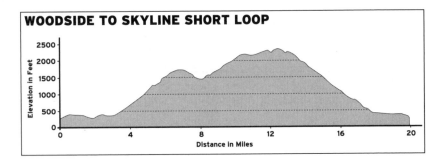

8 WOODSIDE TO COAST LONG LOOP
Woodside to Pescadero

PAVED ROADS WITH MODERATE CAR TRAFFIC

Difficulty: 5

Total Distance: 57.1 miles

Riding Time: 5-7 hours

Elevation Gain: 5,800 feet

Summary: For an epic cycling adventure in the San Francisco Bay Area, this demanding loop can't be beat.

A lot of hill climbing and a lot of scenery make up this all-day ride from Woodside to the coast. With 5,800 feet of elevation gain, it's not for the faint of heart. But there are enough serious cyclists living on the Peninsula that every weekend, hundreds of them take this epic ride, many pedaling in groups of 20 or more.

The ride's first 6.6 miles mimic those of the *Woodside to Skyline Short Loop*, ride 7 in this chapter. But where riders on the short loop head north on Skyline Boulevard, you'll head south, passing by Windy Hill and Russian Ridge Open Space Preserves while gaining another 500 feet, then turn west on Alpine Road. I hope your brakes are in good working order, because you're going to descend 2,000 feet in the next seven miles. Most of it is in open grasslands, but you also pass through a stretch of old-growth redwoods called the Heritage Grove in Alpine Road's last two miles. Lock up your bike and take a short walk through these magnificent trees.

© ANN MARIE BROWN

A cycling club gathers on Skyline Boulevard after the climb from Woodside.

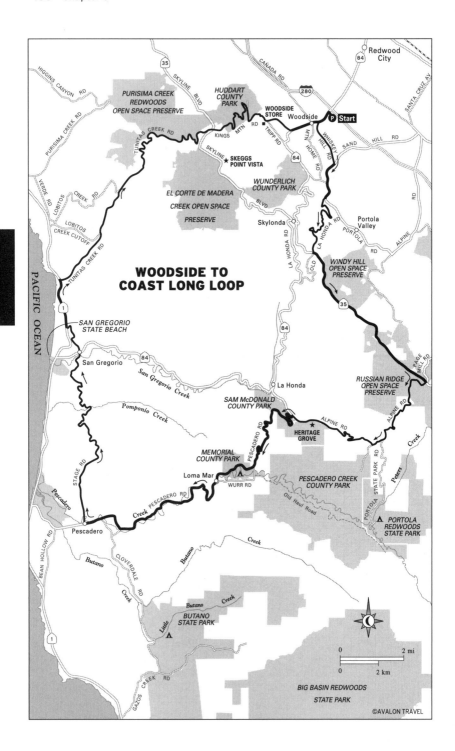

With a left turn on Pescadero Road, you'll climb again over a steep grade for almost two miles, which seems like a heart-breaking injustice. But then you drop again, this time all the way to sea level in the town of Pescadero. After a food and rest break in this small village (there's so much good stuff to eat in a two-block stretch of this tiny village, it's hard to get back on your bike and ride), Stage Road and Highway 1 take you over comparatively easy terrain (two 300-foot climbs) to Tunitas Creek Road, where you will begin your last major climb of the day. If you didn't stop in Pescadero, make sure you do so at the San Gregorio General Store at Highway 84 and Stage Road (650/726-0565, www.sangregoriostore.com), where the ambience will make you feel like you have stepped back in time. Bike shoes are not allowed inside, so be sure to take yours off.

The following ascent, a nine-mile stretch on Tunitas Creek Road, is one of the favorite training rides of cyclists on the coast. Why? Three reasons: The majority of it is in shady redwoods, the climb holds an average 6 percent grade (total 2,000-foot gain), and cars are a rarity.

But wait, this ride's best news is saved for last: The last six miles from Skyline Boulevard are all downhill back to your car. And a well-deserved downhill at that.

Driving Directions

From I-280, take the Highway 84/Woodside exit and drive west for less than 0.25 mile to the Park and Ride lot.

Route Directions

0.0 Park at the Woodside Park and Ride lot. Ride west on Woodside Road (Highway 84). *Supplies are available in Woodside.*

0.5 LEFT on Whiskey Hill Road.

1.8 RIGHT on Sand Hill Road at Y-junction.

3.2 RIGHT on Old La Honda Road.

6.6 LEFT on Skyline Boulevard. *Supplies are available 1.5 miles north (right) in La Honda.*

12.2 RIGHT on Alpine Road.

15.6 RIGHT to stay on Alpine Road.

15.9 RIGHT to stay on Alpine Road.

18.4 Small parking area and hiking trail at Heritage Grove.

19.7 LEFT on Pescadero Road.

20.2 Entrance to Sam McDonald County Park. *Water is available.*

24.1 Entrance to Memorial County Park. *Water is available.*

25.4 Loma Mar Store. *Supplies are available.*

31.5 RIGHT on Stage Road in Pescadero. *Supplies are available in Pescadero.*

38.7 Cross Highway 84 and stay on Stage Road. *Supplies are available at San Gregorio Store.*

39.8 RIGHT on Highway 1.

41.4 RIGHT on Tunitas Creek Road.

43.4 RIGHT at junction with Lobitos Creek Cutoff.

45.0 RIGHT at junction with Lobitos Creek Road.

50.5 Cross Skyline Boulevard and continue on Kings Mountain Road.

53.6 Entrance to Huddart Park on left. *Water is available.*

54.8 LEFT at stop sign at Entrance Way.

55.7 LEFT on Woodside Road (Highway 84).

56.5 Downtown Woodside. *Supplies are available.*

56.6 STRAIGHT at junction with Whiskey Hill Road.

57.1 Arrive at starting point.

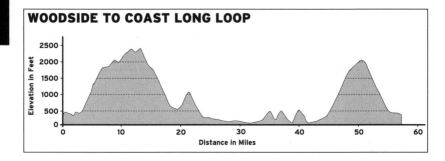

9 RUSSIAN RIDGE AND COAL CREEK LOOP
off Skyline Boulevard near Palo Alto

DIRT ROAD AND SINGLE-TRACK

Difficulty: 2

Riding Time: 1.5 hours

Total Distance: 7.3 miles

Elevation Gain: 800 feet

Summary: The flower-filled days of spring on Skyline Boulevard are ideal for this easy mountain bike ride.

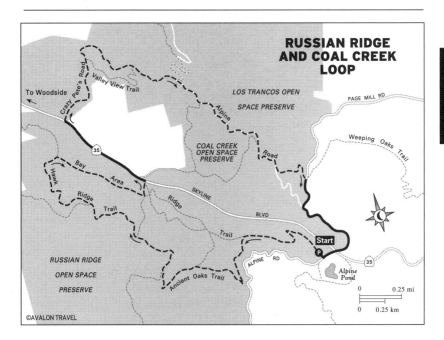

Russian Ridge is one of the few open-space preserves on Skyline Boulevard where beginning mountain bikers have a chance to ride without becoming discouraged by the technical nature of the trails. Conveniently, it's also more than 1,500 acres of windswept ridgetop paradise that will charm you in every season of the year. In summer and fall, the hillsides turn gold and the grasses sway in unison to the ridgetop winds. In winter, the trunks of the moss-covered oaks and laurels turn a bright, verdant green. And in spring, the grasslands explode in a fireworks display of colorful mule's ears, poppies, lupine, goldfields, Johnny-jump-ups, and blue-eyed grass.

This loop route combines a ride through Russian Ridge Open Space Preserve with a ride through neighboring Coal Creek Open Space Preserve, directly across

Russian Ridge Open Space Preserve offers easy-to-moderate trail riding through grasslands and spring wildflowers.

Skyline Boulevard. You'll get to try out your skills on mostly wide fire roads, with a few stints on manageable single-track. This loop is a great place to become more confident on two wheels and at the same time enjoy some beautiful scenery. If you feel like you're getting in over your head at any point, don't be afraid to dismount your bike and walk.

Although each stretch of this loop has its own rewards, a few trails deserve special mention. Ancient Oaks Trail in Russian Ridge is a single-track that leads through a remarkable forest of gnarled, moss-covered oak trees interspersed with equally gnarled Douglas firs, plus some madrones and ferns. You may want to linger for a while in this strange, enchanted woodland. The route also follows a historic road in Coal Creek Open Space Preserve—the old Alpine Road on the east side of Skyline Boulevard, which was closed to cars in the late 1960s. The road was originally built by San Mateo County as a way of encouraging commerce from Santa Cruz County, while bypassing Santa Clara County. (Alpine Road on the west side of Skyline is still open to cars.) The stretch that is covered in this loop—from Crazy Pete's Road to Page Mill Road—looks much more like a trail than a road. It's fun to imagine cars negotiating its narrow turns.

For more information, contact the Midpeninsula Regional Open Space District, 650/691-1200, www.openspace.org.

Driving Directions
From I-280 in Palo Alto, take the Page Mill Road exit west. Drive 8.9 winding

miles to Skyline Boulevard (Highway 35). Cross Skyline Boulevard to Alpine Road. Drive 200 feet on Alpine Road and turn right into the Russian Ridge entrance.

Or, from the junction of Highways 35 and 9 at Saratoga Gap, drive seven miles north on Highway 35 (Skyline Boulevard). Turn left on Alpine Road and then right into the preserve entrance.

Route Directions

0.0 Park at the Russian Ridge main trailhead at Alpine Road and Skyline Boulevard. Ride north on Bay Area Ridge Trail (near restroom). *Supplies are available in Skylonda, 7.5 miles north on Skyline Boulevard.*

0.5 LEFT on connector trail to Ancient Oaks Trail.

0.8 RIGHT on Ancient Oaks Trail.

1.6 RIGHT on Mindego Ridge Trail (wide road).

1.9 STRAIGHT at junction.

2.1 RIGHT on Hawk Trail.

2.7 RIGHT on Bay Area Ridge Trail.

3.2 LEFT to ride out to Skyline Boulevard.

3.3 LEFT (north) on Skyline Boulevard.

4.0 RIGHT on Crazy Pete's Road.

4.4 RIGHT at junction (go through gate).

5.1 RIGHT at junction to stay on Crazy Pete's Road.

5.4 RIGHT on old Alpine Road.

6.5 RIGHT on Page Mill Road (paved road).

7.1 Cross Skyline Boulevard to Alpine Road.

7.2 RIGHT into trailhead parking area.

7.3 Arrive at starting point.

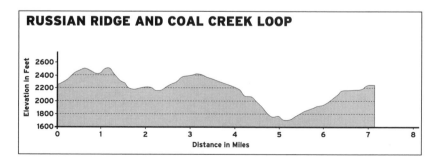

RUSSIAN RIDGE AND COAL CREEK LOOP

10 STANFORD AND PORTOLA VALLEY LOOP
Palo Alto to Portola Valley

PAVED ROADS WITH MODERATE CAR TRAFFIC

Difficulty: 2   **Total Distance:** 18 miles

Riding Time: 1.5 hours   **Elevation Gain:** 750 feet

Summary: For Stanford Cardinal fans, or any cyclist who finds him or herself in the Palo Alto area, this popular exercise ride circles the famous university.

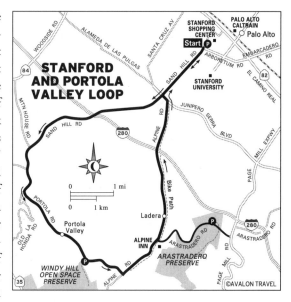

This road ride is more urban than many others in this book, yet it covers some of the most bicycled territory in the Peninsula, the site of millions of after-work or in-between-classes rides. On "The Loop," as it's known, you'll find cyclists at every hour of any day working off a little stress from their high-tech jobs or harried Stanford studies. If you choose to ride your mountain bike here, you can take off from the paved roads onto dirt trails in Arastradero Preserve and/or Windy Hill Open Space Preserve.

Cyclists start this ride from all over the Stanford and Palo Alto area; for convenience, this route begins at the Stanford Shopping Center. If you feel daunted by the first stint on busy Sand Hill Road's bike lane, fear not; you'll soon reach a much quieter stretch on Portola Road and Alpine Road.

In addition, I've added to the traditional loop a peaceful, two-mile, country-lane stretch on Arastradero Road, passing the grassy hills of Arastradero Preserve. This out-and-back begins at the historic Alpine Inn (650/854-4004), formerly Rossotti's (also known as Zot's), reputed to be the oldest roadhouse in continuous operation in California. In the late 1800s, officials at Stanford tried to have the drinking and gambling establishment shut down, fearing its bad influence on

© ANN MARIE BROWN

The popular Alpine Inn is a cyclist's landmark on the Stanford and Portola Valley Loop.

students. They didn't succeed, and, of course, the Alpine Inn has been a popular Stanford beer-and-burger hangout ever since.

On the return leg on Alpine Road, you can opt to pick up the recreation trail that runs alongside the road, starting just past Los Trancos Road. The paved surface is a bit rough, however, so many cyclists stick to the wide shoulder of Alpine Road.

Options

When you ride through the pleasant, small town of Portola Valley, you might want to stop to see the little red Portola schoolhouse next to the town hall and library. Built in 1909, it now serves as an art gallery. The dirt trails of Windy Hill Open Space Preserve are also accessible from the roadside parking lot in Portola Valley (mile 7.6).

Driving Directions

From I-280 in Woodside, take the Sand Hill Road exit and drive east 2.8 miles to Arboretum Road and the Stanford Shopping Center.

Route Directions

0.0 Park at the Stanford Shopping Center near the junction of Arboretum Road and Sand Hill Road (near Nordstrom's). Ride west on the Sand Hill Road bike lane. *Supplies are available in Stanford Shopping Center.*

2.8 Cross under I-280.

5.1 Sand Hill Road becomes Portola Road (stay straight).

7.6 Parking area on right for Windy Hill Open Space Preserve in Portola Valley. *Mountain bikers can ride trails here.*

8.4 LEFT on Alpine Road. *Café and stores available at this junction.*

9.5 RIGHT on Arastradero Road; the Alpine Inn is immediately on the right. *Food and drinks are available at the Alpine Inn.*

10.9 Arastradero Preserve on left (main entrance). *Mountain bikers can ride trails here.*

11.5 Arastradero Road ends at Page Mill Road. TURN AROUND.

13.5 RIGHT on Alpine Road (back at Alpine Inn).

15.3 Cross under I-280.

16.5 STRAIGHT at stoplight onto Santa Cruz Avenue.

16.6 RIGHT on Sand Hill Road.

18.0 Arrive at starting point.

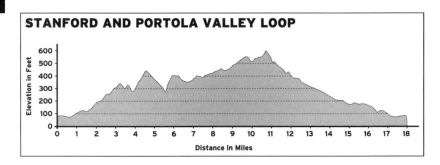

STANFORD AND PORTOLA VALLEY LOOP

11 PESCADERO AND SAN GREGORIO LOOP

BEST [

San Mateo County coast, south of Half Moon Bay

PAVED ROADS WITH MODERATE CAR TRAFFIC

Difficulty: 3	**Total Distance:** 28.7 miles
Riding Time: 2 hours	**Elevation Gain:** 1,200 feet

Summary: Two of San Mateo County's most charming towns and the historic Pigeon Point Lighthouse are visited on this coastal back road loop.

There's one rule about riding coastal Highway 1 south of Half Moon Bay: Ride south, not north, to avoid an often ferocious headwind. This loop around the town of Pescadero allows you to experience the best of Highway 1—heading in the direction of the prevailing winds, while riding on the ocean side of the highway in the safety of a mercifully wide shoulder. The return leg of the loop traces an inland route on mellow country lanes.

Early morning or weekday rides are recommended to avoid potentially heavy beach traffic. This loop makes a great Sunday morning ride with an early start, with time allotted for coffee or breakfast stops in the charming towns of Pescadero and San Gregorio.

Although the mileage isn't high, three long, slow hills in the first six miles of Highway 1 will give you a workout. (Two more hills await on Stage Road, plus one on Cloverdale Road.) The coastal scenery on the first half of the loop is as good as it gets, with nearly nonstop views of the surging sea pounding against a rocky shoreline. A highlight is a visit to Pigeon Point Lighthouse, built in 1871 and now operated as an overnight hostel. Lighthouse tours are often available on weekends for a small fee, but you can always enjoy the views from the lighthouse grounds, and the windswept coast at neighboring Whaler's Cove.

Pigeon Point Lighthouse, built in 1871, is one of the highlights of the Pescadero and San Gregorio Loop.

© ANN MARIE BROWN

Heading south from the lighthouse, you'll turn inland at Gazos Creek Road and enjoy a rolling ride through rural coastal hills. Pedaling north toward Pescadero, you'll pass by the entrance road to Butano State Park, a pretty redwood park with a campground and hiking trails. If you have energy to burn, it's worth a ride in for a look.

In the small town of Pescadero, historic Duarte's Tavern (202 Stage Rd., 650/879-0464, www.duartestavern. com) is a favorite breakfast and lunch stop for cyclists, and two nearby markets sell fresh-baked breads and other goodies. The ride concludes with a 7.2-mile stint on Stage Road, which, before Highway 1 was built, was the only route from Pescadero to San Gregorio.

For more information, contact Pigeon Point Lighthouse, 650/879-2120, www.parks.ca.gov; or Butano State Park, 650/879-2040, www.parks. ca.gov.

Driving Directions

From Highway 1 in Half Moon Bay, drive south for 13 miles to San Gregorio State Beach, just south of the junction with Highway 84. Park in the state beach parking lot.

Route Directions

0.0 Park at San Gregorio State Beach and turn right out of the lot, heading south on Highway 1. *Supplies are available in Half Moon Bay,*

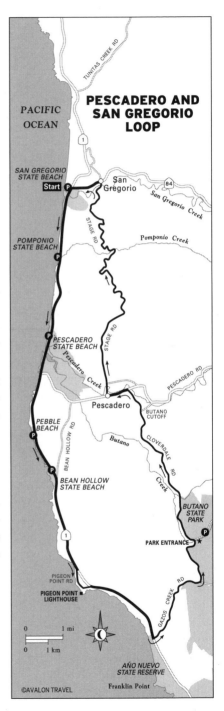

13 miles north on Highway 1, or in San Gregorio, 0.75 mile east on Highway 84.

1.6 Pomponio State Beach.

3.5 Pescadero State Beach and Pescadero Marsh.

4.5 STRAIGHT at junction with Pescadero Road.

6.1 Pebble Beach.

7.0 Bean Hollow State Beach.

9.4 RIGHT on Pigeon Point Road; seaside riding on a quiet access road.

10.1 Pigeon Point Lighthouse. *Lighthouse tours are sometimes available on weekends.*

10.3 RIGHT on Highway 1.

12.5 LEFT on Gazos Creek Road. *Supplies are available at store 50 yards south on Highway 1.*

14.6 LEFT on Cloverdale Road.

15.8 Butano State Park turnoff on the right.

20.1 LEFT on Pescadero Road.

20.6 RIGHT on Stage Road. *Supplies are available in Pescadero (two blocks of shops).*

27.8 LEFT on La Honda Road. *Supplies are available at San Gregorio Store, straight ahead at intersection.*

28.5 LEFT on Highway 1.

28.7 Arrive at starting point.

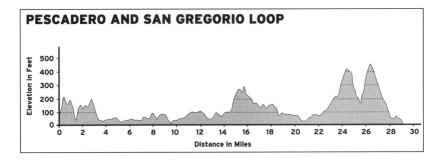

PESCADERO AND SAN GREGORIO LOOP

12 OLD HAUL ROAD LOOP

Pescadero Creek County Park, Loma Mar

DIRT ROAD AND PAVED ROADS WITH MINIMAL CAR TRAFFIC

Difficulty: 3   **Total Distance:** 17.6 miles (or 10-mile option)

Riding Time: 3 hours   **Elevation Gain:** 2,100 feet

Summary: A redwood-lined old railroad bed serves as the basis for this scenic loop on San Mateo County's back roads.

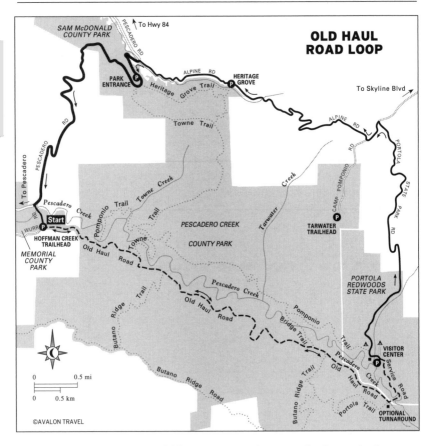

The Old Haul Road is an old logging route that runs for five miles between Pescadero Creek County Park and Portola Redwoods State Park. The historic railroad bed tunnels through a thick forest of second-growth redwoods, providing a smooth, easy ride that gains only 500 feet in elevation. Although plenty of beginning mountain bikers simply pedal it out-and-back, those who want a more strenuous ride with greater variety can use the Old Haul Road to connect to paved Portola State Park Road and Alpine Road, home of the awe-inspiring Heritage Grove of old-growth redwoods.

On the Pescadero Creek County Park side, the Old Haul Road starts by a small picnic area near the rushing creek gorge, then heads east. You'll see plenty of big stumps along the route—reminders of this forest's earlier state—and many tiny streams that run down the hillsides to empty into Pescadero Creek. The hard-packed dirt-and-gravel road is well signed and easy to follow the whole way. Your only concern is to watch out for equestrians and hikers, who also use this trail.

Once you reach the Old Haul Road's terminus at Portola Redwoods State Park, you face a long, slow climb of 900 feet over four miles on the park's paved

Mountain bikers can ride an easy out-and-back trail on Old Haul Road or do a more strenuous loop.

entrance road. It is followed by a long, fast descent on Alpine Road to the Heritage Grove. After enjoying the grandeur of the mighty trees, you face a second climb, this time with a steeper grade, as Pescadero Road ascends mercilessly for just under two miles. (Prepare to use your granny gear.) The last two miles are an easy downhill cruise back to your car. Although the roads on this loop are quite narrow, they get little traffic, so you won't have to worry much about cars.

For more information, contact San Mateo County Parks and Recreation, 650/363-4020, www.eparks.net; or Portola Redwoods State Park, 650/948-9098, www.santacruzstateparks.org.

Options

If you want to get a novice hooked on mountain biking, take them for a 10-mile out-and-back ride on the Old Haul Road.

Driving Directions

From Highway 1, 15 miles south of Half Moon Bay, drive east on Pescadero Road for 9.8 miles. Turn right at the second entrance to Wurr Road, 0.25 mile past the entrance to Memorial Park. Drive 0.25 mile to the Hoffman Creek Trailhead, where Old Haul Road begins. (Or, from I-280 at Woodside, take Highway 84 west for 13 miles to La Honda. Turn left on Pescadero Road and drive 1 mile, then bear right to stay on Pescadero Road. Continue 4.2 miles to Wurr Road on the left. Turn left and drive 0.25 mile to the trailhead.)

Route Directions

0.0 Park at the Wurr Road entrance to Pescadero Creek County Park. Begin riding at the entrance gate. *Supplies are available at the Loma Mar Store, 1.5 miles west on Pescadero Road.*

0.5 STRAIGHT at junction with Pomponio Trail.

1.1 STRAIGHT at junction with Towne Trail.

3.2 Reach high point in the trail and start to descend.

3.9 STRAIGHT at junction with Bridge Trail on left and Butano Ridge Trail on right.

5.0 LEFT at service road to Portola Redwoods State Park; descend and continue past the gate onto paved road.

6.0 Portola State Park visitor center and restrooms on the left. *Water is available.*

6.4 Exit out of Portola State Park and follow Portola State Park Road.

9.3 LEFT on Alpine Road.

9.6 RIGHT to stay on Alpine Road.

12.1 Heritage Grove. *Take a short walk through these magnificent trees.*

13.3 LEFT on Pescadero Road.

13.8 Entrance to Sam McDonald County Park. *Water is available.*

17.4 LEFT on Wurr Road.

17.6 Arrive at starting point.

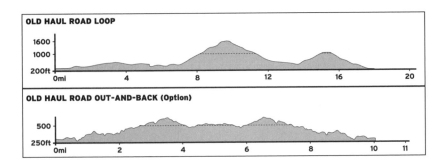

🔳 BIG BASIN AND BOULDER CREEK LOOP

Santa Cruz Mountains and Big Basin Redwoods State Park

PAVED ROADS WITH MODERATE CAR TRAFFIC

Difficulty: 4

Riding Time: 3-4 hours

Total Distance: 43 miles

Elevation Gain: 3,300 feet

Summary: This road ride winds through one of the least developed regions of the South Bay, from the redwoods of Big Basin to the vineyards of Bear Creek Road.

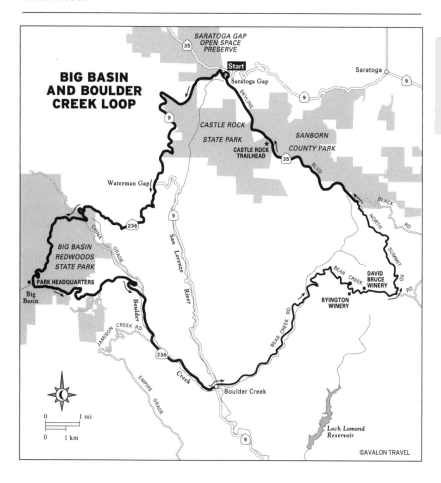

A shoulderless stretch of Highway 9 leads to Big Basin Redwoods State Park.

This road ride explores the ridges and forests of the Santa Cruz Mountains and includes a visit to California's first state park, Big Basin Redwoods. You'll see plenty of redwoods along the route, plus ridgeline forests of madrone and oak. Long climbs and descents are part of the package, and you'll have to put up with auto traffic on narrow, shoulder-less roads. But it's worth it to complete this 43-mile epic trip through some of the South Bay's most remote countryside.

The loop ride begins at Saratoga Gap at the junction of Highway 9 and Skyline Boulevard (Highway 35) and heads southwest to Big Basin Redwoods State Park. A 6-mile descent from Saratoga Gap at 2,634 feet to Waterman Gap at 1,267 feet is your warm-up for the day. Continuing straight on narrow, twisting Highway 236, you'll face a moderate up-and-down ride to state park headquarters. Lock up your bike at the parking lot and take the 0.5-mile walk on Redwood Trail, which shows off some of the park's largest and oldest redwoods, including the Mother of the Forest (329 feet tall) and the Santa Clara Tree (17 feet in diameter). Nothing compares to the humbling feeling of walking in the shadows of 2,000-year-old giants.

Back on your bike, you'll exit the park and continue south on Highway 236, climbing briefly and then dropping down to the town of Boulder Creek. After a food and rest stop, and maybe a triple espresso, you face a strenuous climb from Boulder Creek (500 feet in elevation) to North Summit Road near Los Gatos (2,200 feet in elevation). You'll pass two wineries along the way. Byington Vineyard (408/354-1111, www.byington.com) offers wine tastings Tuesday–Sunday 11 A.M.–5 P.M., picnic facilities, and a bocce ball court. David Bruce Winery (408/354-4214, www.davidbrucewinery.com) holds wine tastings Thursday–Monday noon–5 P.M.

If you can somehow pull yourself through this unforgiving stretch (and no, a little wine won't help), the remaining miles on narrow North Summit Road and Skyline Boulevard will seem relatively easy. Thankfully, the last two miles on Skyline Boulevard to your car at Saratoga Gap are actually downhill.

For more information, contact Big Basin Redwoods State Park, 831/338-8860, www.santacruzstateparks.org.

Driving Directions

From I-280 in Palo Alto, take Page Mill Road west for 8.9 miles to Skyline Boulevard (Highway 35). Turn left (south) on Skyline and drive 10.5 miles to the junction with Highway 9. The parking lot is on the left. Or, from Saratoga, take Highway 9 west for 7.5 miles to its junction with Skyline Boulevard.

Route Directions

0.0 Park at the large parking lot at the junction of Highway 9 and Highway 35. Ride west on Highway 9. *A vendor sells hot dogs and drinks in the parking lot on most weekends. Other supplies are available in Saratoga.*

1.8 Overlook point and restrooms on left.

6.1 RIGHT on Highway 236 at Waterman Gap.

10.8 STRAIGHT at junction with China Grade.

14.2 Big Basin Redwoods State Park headquarters. *Lock up your bike and take a hike on the 0.5-mile Redwood Trail from the main parking lot. Water, restrooms, and a small store are available (open most of the year).*

20.6 Pass golf course.

23.5 LEFT onto Highway 9 at stop sign. *Supplies are available in town of Boulder Creek.*

23.6 RIGHT on Bear Creek Road.

28.3 Begin major climb.

31.0 Byington Vineyard & Winery on right.

31.6 David Bruce Winery on left.

32.6 LEFT on North Summit Road (unsigned except for the spray-painted word Skyline and an arrow); end of major climb.

36.5 STRAIGHT at junction with Black Road; North Summit Road widens and becomes Skyline Boulevard.

40.4 Castle Rock State Park entrance.

43.0 Arrive at starting point.

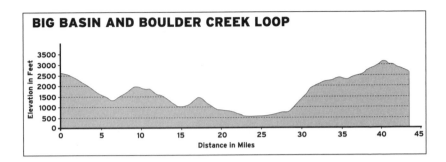

14 SARATOGA GAP LOOP BEST 【

off Skyline Boulevard near Saratoga

DIRT ROAD AND SINGLE-TRACK

Difficulty: 3 **Total Distance:** 12.9 miles

Riding Time: 2-3 hours **Elevation Gain:** 1,600 feet

Summary: Hone your mountain bike skills on a deservedly popular loop of mostly single-track riding through three separate Skyline-area parks.

When I was first getting acquainted with mountain biking, I met a pro rider on the trail who gave me one piece of advice: "If you want to learn how to handle single-track, ride Saratoga Gap Trail—often."

It was sage advice. I'm still not the world's greatest single-track rider (not even close), but I know where to go to sharpen my skills.

So does everyone else. This loop is one of the most popular in the South Bay, and for good reason. It starts at the busy junction of Highways 9 and 35, with easy access from most of Silicon Valley and the Peninsula, and carves its way through three separate parks and preserves: Saratoga Gap, Long Ridge, and Upper Stevens Creek.

The loop can be ridden in only one direction because one leg is open to uphill traffic only. If you can take your eyes off the six-foot space in front of your front tire, you'll find that the surrounding foothill scenery is lovely: open grassland ridges, fern-filled forests of handsome Douglas firs, wide views of wooded hillsides, and even a visit to a trickling creek in Stevens Canyon, which makes a perfect mid-loop rest stop.

The ride through Long Ridge Open Space Preserve is one of the easier stretches of the Saratoga Gap Loop.

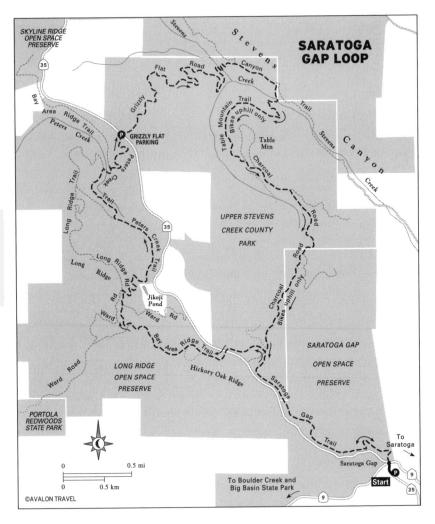

Aside from the technical challenges of single-track on Saratoga Gap, Peters Creek, and Table Mountain Trails, the only major difficulty on this ride is the long climb out on Charcoal Road, a 1.3-mile workout. But since it is preceded by a steep descent on Grizzly Flat Road to Stevens Canyon, you are clearly forewarned that the uphill is coming. More than a few riders have been spotted walking their bikes here.

Note that this is a dry-season-only loop; many of the trails are closed during wet weather. Please don't ride them illegally.

For more information, contact Midpeninsula Regional Open Space District, 650/691-1200, www.openspace.org.

Driving Directions

From I-280 in Palo Alto, take Page Mill Road west for 8.9 miles to Skyline Boulevard (Highway 35). Turn left (south) on Skyline and drive 10.5 miles to the junction with Highway 9. The parking lot is on the left. Or, from Saratoga, take Highway 9 west for 7.5 miles to its junction with Skyline Boulevard.

Route Directions

0.0 Park at the large parking lot at the junction of Highway 9 and Highway 35. Ride across Highway 9 carefully to access Saratoga Gap Trail. *A vendor sells hot dogs and drinks in the parking lot on most weekends. Other supplies are available in Saratoga.*

2.0 Single-track Saratoga Gap Trail ends at Highway 35; cross the highway and go RIGHT on Bay Area Ridge Trail.

3.2 RIGHT on single-track (signed for Grizzly Flat parking).

3.3 STRAIGHT at junction with Ward Road on left.

3.4 RIGHT on single-track Peters Creek Trail at major junction of Ward Road, Long Ridge Road, and Peters Creek Trail.

4.3 RIGHT to stay on Peters Creek Trail. Keep to right at next two forks to come out to Highway 35.

5.3 Cross Highway 35 and pick up Grizzly Flat Road on other side; steep and long descent.

7.8 Cross Stevens Creek.

8.0 RIGHT on Canyon Trail.

8.3 RIGHT on Table Mountain Trail (single-track signed To Saratoga Gap).

9.5 RIGHT on Table Mountain Trail/Charcoal Road (wide road).

9.9 RIGHT on Charcoal Road; begin major hill climb.

10.4 RIGHT to stay on Charcoal Road.

11.2 LEFT at junction with Saratoga Gap Trail. *Check out the Miwok grinding stones near this junction.*

12.9 Arrive at starting point.

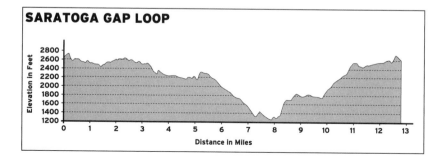

15 MONTE BELLO LOOP
Saratoga to Monte Bello Ridge

DIRT ROAD AND SINGLE-TRACK; PAVED ROADS WITH MODERATE CAR TRAFFIC

Difficulty: 4   **Total Distance:** 27 miles (or 21.2-mile option)

Riding Time: 3 hours   **Elevation Gain:** 2,300 feet

Summary: Views from Monte Bello's high ridge and a picnic at Ridge Winery are your rewards for a serious climb from downtown Saratoga.

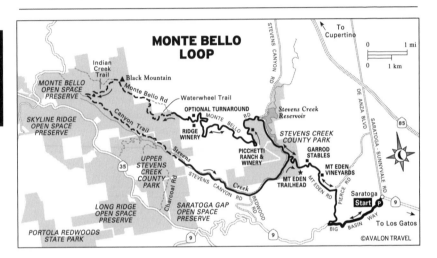

The roads around Stevens Creek Reservoir and throughout Stevens Creek Canyon are well traveled by cyclists from the Silicon Valley every day of the week. The proximity of this lovely, tree-lined canyon to the hustle and bustle of Cupertino makes it perfect for after-work, lunchtime, and weekend rides.

The ride described here is designed to allow for the most scenery with the least traffic. The route travels up Pierce Road from Saratoga through a mix of vineyards, red-tile-roofed mansions, and older farmhouses, then cruises through the foothills of Mount Eden Road and creekside Stevens Canyon Road to Monte Bello Road. Following this path, you'll encounter two brief climbs, then nothing but climbing on Monte Bello's increasingly narrow road. The road gains 1,500 feet over 4.3 miles, with grades occasionally as steep as 13 percent.

Achieving Monte Bello's high ridge is your reward, with its spreading views overlooking the Santa Clara Valley and a chance for wine-tasting and a picnic at Ridge Winery (weekends only). Skinny-tire riders can continue for another mile beyond the vineyards to where the pavement ends, but then they'll have to turn

Bikes of all shapes and sizes can be ridden to the summit of Monte Bello Road.

around (see *Options*). Mountain bikers stay on Monte Bello Road to the Waterwheel Creek Trail in Monte Bello Open Space Preserve, then follow that trail to the dirt section of Monte Bello Road. Shortly, you're at the microwave-covered summit of 2,800-foot Black Mountain, the highest point on Monte Bello Ridge. Views are good in all directions, but the best vista is to the west, as seen from near the 15-mph speed limit sign at an obvious outcrop of scattered rocks: Stevens Creek Canyon lies below you. Untrammeled grassland hills spread to the north and south along Skyline Ridge. The Pacific Ocean glimmers from afar. In springtime, the grassland wildflowers explode in a riot of colors.

The all-dirt downhill is exciting and fast; be careful not to mow over cyclists riding in the opposite direction. Indian Creek Trail drops 850 feet over 1.2 miles, then Canyon Trail descends almost as fast, adding a little single-track to the mix. Where the dirt ends, you follow paved Stevens Canyon Road to Mount Eden Road, then retrace your tracks to Saratoga.

If you're out on Sunday, you may be able to stop after your ride at the Picchetti Winery for a well-deserved rest and some live music. The winery (408/741-1310, www.picchetti.com) is located at 13100 Monte Bello Road. Ridge Winery (408/867-3233, www.ridgewine.com) is located at 17100 Monte Bello Road.

For more information on Monte Bello Open Space Preserve, contact Midpeninsula Regional Open Space District, 650/691-1200, www.openspace.org.

Options

Road cyclists can enjoy a 21.2-mile out-and-back on pavement by following this same route up to Ridge Winery, then retracing their tire treads. The route has a 2,000-foot elevation gain.

Driving Directions

From San Jose, take Highway 17 south for 6 miles to the Highway 9 exit in Los Gatos. Take Highway 9 northwest 2.5 miles into Saratoga and park in downtown.

Route Directions

0.0 Park in downtown Saratoga in any of the public parking lots one block off Highway 9. Ride west on Highway 9. *Supplies are available in Saratoga.*

1.6 RIGHT on Pierce Road (signed for Mountain Winery).

2.6 LEFT on Mount Eden Road.

3.1 Mount Eden Vineyards.

3.5 Garrod Farm Stables.

4.1 Mount Eden Trailhead on the left (no bikes).

4.9 STRAIGHT on Stevens Canyon Road at stop sign.

6.3 LEFT on Monte Bello Road.

6.8 Picchetti Ranch and Winery at Monte Bello Open Space Preserve (live music on Sunday).

8.3 Road narrows considerably.

10.6 Ridge Winery on the left. *Wine-tasting on weekends; restrooms and water are available.*

11.5 LEFT on Waterwheel Creek Trail (gated dirt trail).

12.9 LEFT on Monte Bello Road (dirt).

13.8 Summit of Black Mountain.

14.1 LEFT on Indian Creek Trail.

15.0 LEFT on Canyon Trail, stay left at next two junctions to stay on Canyon Trail.

18.5 Gate and start of Stevens Canyon Road.

20.4 LEFT to stay on Stevens Canyon Road.

22.1 RIGHT on Mount Eden Road.

27.0 Arrive at starting point.

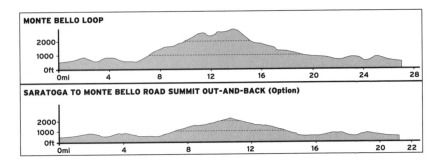

16 COYOTE CREEK TRAIL

San Jose to Morgan Hill

PAVED BIKE PATH

Difficulty: 2

Riding Time: 2-3 hours

Total Distance: 29.4 miles

Elevation Gain: 400 feet

Summary: This paved recreation trail starts at San Jose's velodrome and is long enough to rack up some serious training miles.

Think San Jose and you probably think industrial parks. It's true, San Jose has more than its share of these mammoth concrete complexes, but it also has peaceful farmlands, orchards, and gurgling creeks. The Coyote Creek Trail passes by all of these on its 14.7-mile length from Coyote Hellyer County Park south to Anderson Lake County Park. This makes a level, 29.4-mile round-trip on a paved recreation trail. If you simply want to crank out some level miles on your bike without worrying about cars or trail junctions, this is a good place to do it, and it's close to home for millions of Bay Area residents.

The trail begins at Coyote Hellyer County

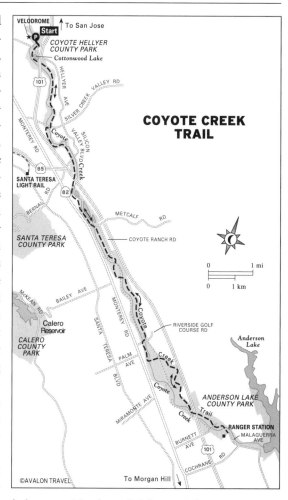

Park, home of the only velodrome in Northern California. Bike races are usually held on Wednesday, Thursday, and Friday nights in summer. The open-air velodrome was built in 1962 as a training site for the Pan American Games. A single lap around the track is 335 meters, or about 0.2 mile, and the corners are sharply banked. If you've never watched bike racing in a velodrome, you have to check it out.

In the trail's first 0.5 mile, you'll ride past small Cottonwood Lake on the left, a popular spot with shore anglers. The lake, which was developed out of an old rock quarry, is stocked with rainbow trout. Shortly beyond it, the trail crosses under U.S. 101 to the highway's east side. You'll cross the highway twice more along the route.

As you ride, ignore the numerous side bridges over Coyote Creek that access San Jose neighborhoods. Stay on the main path, which for a paved trail is a bit rough in places. You'll have to put up with the steady hum of road noise from U.S. 101 and Monterey Highway, which are never far away. But you'll also have the fine companionship of shady sycamores, cottonwoods, and live oaks along Coyote Creek, plus occasional scrub jays and ground squirrels. South of Metcalf Road, an equestrian trail parallels the paved trail, so you may see some horses, too.

The trail ends by the ranger station at Anderson Lake County Park, site of Santa Clara County's largest reservoir. You might want to lock up your bike here and take a walk on the one-mile, self-guided nature trail that runs to Malaguerra Avenue. It, too, follows Coyote Creek; a printed trail guide interprets the creek's riparian habitat.

For more information, contact Santa Clara County Parks and Recreation Department, 408/355-2200 or 408/225-0225, www.parkhere.org.

Options
If you've ever dreamed of riding on a velodrome track, your dreams can come true at Hellyer Park. Beginner sessions are held every Saturday morning. You can rent a fixed-gear track bike and will receive basic track instruction, all for about $10. For more information, visit www.ridethetrack.com.

Driving Directions
From San Jose, drive 4 miles south on U.S. 101 and take the Hellyer Avenue exit. Drive 0.25 mile to the Coyote Hellyer County Park entrance. Just beyond the entrance kiosk, bear left at the fork and park at the velodrome parking lot.

Route Directions
  0.0 Park at the velodrome parking lot. The bike path begins by the restrooms. *Water is available at the park.*

  0.4 Cottonwood Lake on the left.

0.8 Cross under U.S. 101.

3.0 LEFT at tricky intersection on far side of bridge.

5.5 Cross under U.S. 101.

6.8 Cross Metcalf Road to Coyote Ranch Road; go right to continue on path.

7.7 LEFT on Coyote Ranch Road, then RIGHT back onto path.

10.6 Cross Riverside Golf Course road.

14.0 Cross under U.S. 101.

14.7 Arrive at the ranger station for Anderson Lake County Park. TURN AROUND. *Water is available at the park.*

29.4 Arrive at starting point.

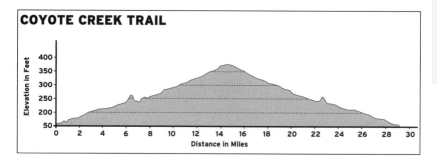

 MOUNT HAMILTON

BEST ◖

Joseph D. Grant County Park, southeast of San Jose

PAVED ROAD WITH MINIMAL CAR TRAFFIC

Difficulty: 4   **Total Distance:** 23 miles (or longer options)

Riding Time: 2 hours   **Elevation Gain:** 2,700 feet

Summary: Put your granny gear to work on this strenuous climb to the top of the Bay Area's loftiest peak.

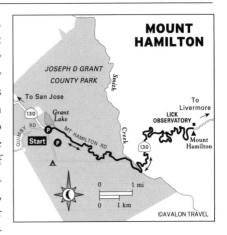

The summit of Mount Hamilton, at 4,209 feet, is high enough so that on those rare winter days when snow falls in the Bay Area, it is gloriously crowned in white. It's the Bay Area's loftiest peak, and the highest you can drive to—or ride your bike to. It's also the home of Lick Observatory, where astronomers from the University of California keep a watch on the stars. Constructed in 1887 by James Lick, the observatory was once famous for its 36-inch telescope, the world's largest at that time.

The ascent to Mount Hamilton's summit is challenging, but not impossibly so, thanks to the curving, twisting, switchbacking, steady 5–7 percent grade of Mount Hamilton Road. Beginning from Joseph D. Grant County Park, you have 11.5 miles to gain 2,700 feet in elevation to the summit (this includes a 300-foot descent to Smith Creek, which you must regain).

Junctions are few and far between on this road, so you don't have route directions to worry about. Just follow the pavement uphill, through a landscape of grasslands, buckeyes, and mistletoe-draped oaks. In spring, the mountain is well known for its wildflower displays, and in autumn, the fall colors on the upper slopes can be delightful. As you ascend the mountain, you'll notice the foliage change: Coulter pines with their big, heavy cones appear among the manzanita, plus leafy black oaks. It gets cooler the higher you go, and the views of Santa Clara Valley get better and better.

For more information, contact Joseph D. Grant County Park, 408/274-6121, www.parkhere.org. The Lick Observatory (408/274-5061, www.ucolick.org) is open daily in summer noon–5 P.M. and Thursday–Sunday in winter noon–5 P.M.

Options

If you want to keep riding beyond the summit, help yourself. San Antonio Valley Road rolls, winds, and gradually descends until it changes names to Mines Road and eventually winds up in Livermore, 45 miles later. Almost no cars travel this stretch of road, so it's all yours. If you happen to know someone in Livermore who will give you a ride back to Joseph Grant Park, you're in for a fine day. Another way to add mileage is to start your ride at the junction of Alum Rock Avenue and Mount Hamilton Road, where there are pullouts on the side of Alum Rock Avenue with space for about 20 cars. This will add another 15.6 miles to your round-trip summit ride.

wild pig warning on Mount Hamilton Road near Lick Observatory

© ANN MARIE BROWN

Driving Directions

From I-680 in San Jose, take the Alum Rock Avenue exit and drive east 2.2 miles. Turn right on Mount Hamilton Road and drive 7.8 miles to the main entrance to Joseph D. Grant County Park on the right. Park in the county park lot (fee charged) or alongside the road in pullouts (no fee).

Route Directions

0.0 Park near the entrance to Joseph D. Grant County Park and ride southeast on Mount Hamilton Road. *Water is available in the park campground; supplies are available in San Jose.*

3.5 Twin Gates Trailhead and start of descent to Smith Creek. *Now or on the return trip, take a walk on Cañada de Pala Trail to see an abundance of blue-eyed grass, Johnny-jump-ups, brodiaea, shooting stars, and goldfields (springtime only).*

4.4 Smith Creek bridge.

5.6 STRAIGHT at junction with Kincaid Road on left.

10.9 RIGHT at Lick Observatory junction.

11.5 Arrive at main building and visitor area of observatory. TURN AROUND. *Water and snack machines are available when the visitor*

center is open, weekday afternoons and weekends 10 A.M.–5 P.M. Public tours are available.

23.0 Arrive at starting point.

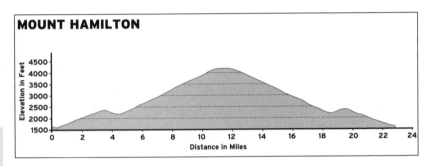

MOUNT HAMILTON

18 GRANT RANCH LOOP

Joseph D. Grant County Park, southeast of San Jose

DIRT ROAD

Difficulty: 3

Riding Time: 2 hours

Total Distance: 10.9 or 12 miles

Elevation Gain: 1,600 feet

Summary: A series of ranch roads carve their way through the grasslands and past magnificent oaks in this pastoral county park.

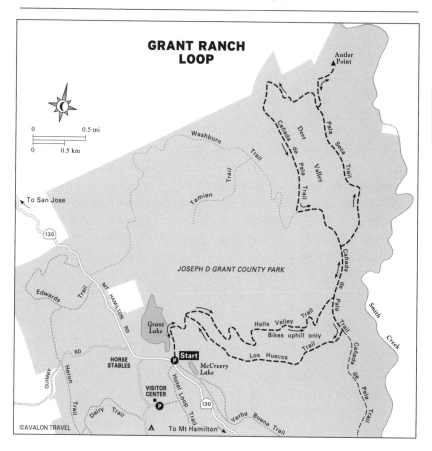

Joseph D. Grant County Park, called Grant Ranch by the locals, lies due north of better known Henry Coe State Park, and it shares the same summer weather—hot as Hades. Plan your trip for the cooler months, preferably April or May when the grasslands are green and the slopes are gilded with wildflowers.

The park's trails are predominantly multiuse dirt roads that are used by mountain

© ANN MARIE BROWN

At Joseph D. Grant County Park, most of the riding is on old ranch roads with steep hills on parts of the trails.

bikers more than anybody else. Almost every trail is an old ranch road, so if you are a single-track snob, you won't be happy here.

This challenging figure-eight loop trip takes you to the highest point in the park, Antler Point at 2,995 feet. The first two miles include some memorably steep up-hill pitches, but the rest of the trip is more moderate. The ride starts at the Grant Lake Trailhead and follows Halls Valley Trail (open to bikes in the uphill direction only). The next 2.1 miles are the toughest of the ride, but as you gain elevation, you also gain surprising views of the South Bay's distant shimmering waters.

Where the trail tops out at Cañada de Pala Trail, turn left and enjoy an easier, more rolling grade. More views of the South Bay are seen to the northwest, and Mount Hamilton shows up to the east. Look for abundant displays of spring wildflowers on this high, bald ridge.

Your destination, Antler Point, is visible straight ahead, the highest hill around. Follow Pala Seca Trail through grasslands and occasional grazing bovines to Antler Point's spur trail. This grassy overlook supplies the day's best view of the South Bay, San Jose, Grant Park's rolling grasslands, and Lick Observatory on top of 4,209-foot Mount Hamilton.

For your return trip, loop back on Cañada de Pala Trail, enjoying more high views. You have some choices for the final leg: Los Huecos Trail (a very fast and steep downhill for a 10.9-mile loop) or Yerba Buena Trail (a more gentle downhill for a 12-mile loop). The latter will get you away from the biking crowds, but if you love screaming downhills, Los Huecos Trail is the only way to go.

For more information, contact Joseph D. Grant County Park, 408/274-6121, www.parkhere.org.

Driving Directions

From I-680 in San Jose, take the Alum Rock Avenue exit and drive east 2.2 miles. Turn right on Mount Hamilton Road and drive 7.8 miles to the sign for Joseph D. Grant County Park on the right. Don't turn here; continue another 100 yards to the Grant Lake parking lot on the left.

Route Directions

0.0 Park at the Grant Lake parking area. Follow the trail to the left to Grant Lake. *Water is available at the park campground.*

0.3 RIGHT on connector trail to Halls Valley Trail.

0.6 Straight on Halls Valley Trail and begin steep climb.

2.7 LEFT on Cañada de Pala Trail.

3.1 RIGHT on Pala Seca Trail.

4.8 RIGHT on Antler Point Trail (walk your bike 0.2 mile uphill to this 2,995-foot viewpoint).

4.9 Arrive at Antler Point. TURN AROUND.

5.1 RIGHT at junction with Pala Seca Trail.

8.1 LEFT to stay on Cañada de Pala Trail.

8.5 RIGHT on Los Huecos Trail; begin fast, steep descent. *If you prefer a gentler descent, continue on Cañada de Pala Trail for 1.3 miles farther and turn right on Yerba Buena Trail; this gets you back to your car in a 12-mile round-trip.*

10.3 STRAIGHT to return to Grant Lake.

10.6 LEFT to return to parking lot.

10.9 Arrive at starting point.

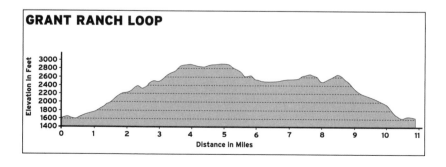

GRANT RANCH LOOP

19 MIDDLE RIDGE LOOP

BEST ◖

Henry W. Coe State Park, east of Morgan Hill

DIRT ROAD AND SINGLE-TRACK

Difficulty: 4

Total Distance: 10.8 miles

Riding Time: 2 hours

Elevation Gain: 2,100 feet

Summary: This huge state park is a great place to get away from it all and enjoy some great single-track riding and steep climbs and descents.

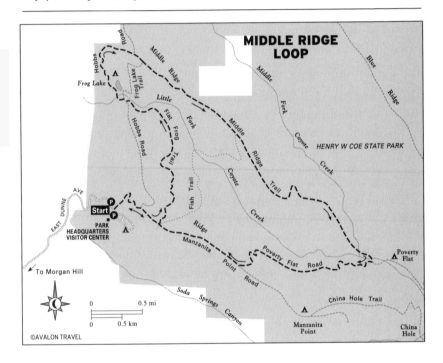

The closest thing to a wilderness park in the South Bay area is Henry W. Coe State Park. This well-known but little-traveled state park is the second largest in California (the largest is Anza-Borrego Desert State Park near San Diego). Composed of tall ridges bisected by deep, steep ravines, the park is notoriously hilly. Its varied terrain includes grasslands, oaks, chaparral, pines, and mixed hardwoods.

Henry Coe is so large—80,000 acres—and its terrain is so rugged that to see much of it, you need to pack your bike's panniers and plan to stay for a few days. But day visitors can tour the western part of the park on this 10.8-mile loop around Middle Ridge. The ride has some of the finest single-track to be found in the

Henry W. Coe State Park provides a challenging single-track ride on the Middle Ridge Loop.

South Bay, but it also has some of the steepest fire road climbs. Come mentally and physically prepared for a workout; this park is not for beginners.

Pick a cool day for the ride, ideally in spring when Coe Park's wildflowers are blooming, or in autumn when the air is clear and cool. The park is extremely hot in summer, and its single-track trails are temporarily closed after winter rainstorms. Also in the rainy months, the wide Middle Fork of Coyote Creek at mile 7.2 may be more than a few feet deep and too dangerous to cross. Check with rangers before riding this loop after a period of rain.

The first leg of the ride follows Flat Frog Trail, a pleasant single-track that leads through a mixed woodland of ponderosa pines, black oaks, and madrones. The trail connects with Hobbs Road just before Frog Lake; take the steep ranch road to the former cattle pond. (A backpacking camp is located nearby.) Tiny Frog Lake is spring fed; it supports a few bass and bluegill. Frequently, the surface of the water is completely covered with green algae. Cross Frog Lake's inlet and continue steeply uphill to Middle Ridge. The oak-dotted grasslands above Frog Lake support colorful wildflowers, which give you something to look at while you stop to catch your breath.

Once you reach Middle Ridge, look forward to a roller-coaster descent with many fine views of Coyote Creek canyon. Although Middle Ridge Trail initially leads through alternating grassy clearings and groves of pines and black oaks, it later enters a grove of giant, tree-sized manzanitas growing 15 feet tall. The trail loses 1,700 feet over 3.4 miles (with one short but steep uphill), and becomes more technical as it drops. In its final mile, it is downright treacherous—steep, loose, narrow, rocky, and rutted.

After crossing the Middle Fork of Coyote Creek, get ready to pay the price for all the fun you've had: You face a 1.8-mile climb on rocky Poverty Flat Road with a 1,400-foot elevation gain (12 percent average grade). Sometimes mountain biking is hell, and this is one of those times. When at last you reach Manzanita Point Road, the punishment is over, and you have an easy ride back to your car.

For more information, contact Henry W. Coe State Park, 408/779-2728, www. coepark.org.

Driving Directions

From U.S. 101 in Morgan Hill, take the East Dunne Avenue exit and drive east for 13 miles to Henry W. Coe State Park headquarters.

Route Directions

0.0 Park at the lot near park headquarters. Follow paved Manzanita Point Road from near the headquarters building (pavement ends shortly). *Water is available at the trailhead; supplies are available in Morgan Hill.*

0.5 RIGHT to stay on Manzanita Point Road at junction with Hobbs Road.

0.7 LEFT on Flat Frog Trail.

2.9 RIGHT on Hobbs Road.

3.2 Frog Lake. Cross the dam and join trail to Middle Ridge (steep climb uphill).

3.8 RIGHT on Middle Ridge Trail; begin long, steep descent.

5.1 STRAIGHT on Middle Ridge Trail at junction with Fish Trail.

7.2 Cross Middle Fork of Coyote Creek at Poverty Flat.

7.3 RIGHT on Poverty Flat Road; begin long, steep climb out.

9.1 RIGHT on Manzanita Point Road.

10.3 LEFT to stay on Manzanita Point Road.

10.8 Arrive at starting point.

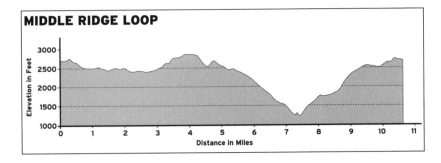

20 BERRY CREEK FALLS BIKE AND HIKE (SKYLINE-TO-THE-SEA TRAIL)   BEST 🌙
Big Basin Redwoods State Park, south of Pescadero

DIRT ROAD AND SINGLE-TRACK

Difficulty: 2   **Total Distance:** 11.6 miles (plus 1.2-mile hike)

Riding Time: 2.5 hours   **Elevation Gain:** 550 feet

Summary: Take a jaunt to one of the Bay Area's prettiest waterfalls by bike and on foot, easy enough for the whole family to enjoy.

You can see Berry Creek Falls the hard way, by hiking 5.5 hilly miles from park headquarters at Big Basin Redwoods State Park, or you can see Berry Creek Falls the easy way, by riding your bike 5.8 nearly level miles from the coast near Davenport, then walking the last 0.6 mile.

The 70-foot falls are worth seeing no matter how you get there, but if you have children in tow, or if you aren't anywhere near the Boulder Creek entrance to the park, or if you'd just rather ride than walk, the bike route is a smart choice. Riders of almost any ability can handle the wide dirt road, and the trip begins and ends at an easy-access trailhead right on Highway 1.

The trail, which is the western section of the 38-mile-long Skyline-to-the-Sea Trail, used to be even easier to ride, but a series of heavy rains in the 1990s washed parts of it into Waddell Creek, forcing one stretch to be rerouted as narrow single-track with a few ludicrously tight turns. The vast majority of riders simply walk their bikes through this 100-yard stretch.

The old ranch road begins by the highway, passes by Big Basin's Rancho del Oso visitor center and a few private farms, then enters the redwoods. The entire route parallels Waddell Creek until the final walk to the falls, where the trail follows Berry Creek. Several

An easy ride through the redwoods leads to the beautiful Berry Creek Falls.

© ANN MARIE BROWN

backpacking camps are located a few yards off the route, used mostly by hikers following the entire length of Skyline-to-the-Sea Trail.

Make sure you bring a bike lock so you can secure your wheels at the bike rack and take the 15-minute hike to the waterfall (bikes are not allowed). A bench on the viewing platform at Berry Creek Falls makes a perfect spot for lunch, if it isn't already in use by somebody else. Not surprisingly, this is a popular spot year-round. Plan a weekday trip if at all possible.

For more information, contact Big Basin Redwoods State Park, 831/338-8860, www.santacruzstateparks.org.

Driving Directions

From Half Moon Bay at the junction of Highway 92 and Highway 1, drive south on Highway 1 for 30 miles to the Rancho del Oso area of Big Basin Redwoods State Park (across from Waddell Beach, 7.5 miles north of Davenport). Park on the east side of the highway by the Rancho del Oso gate.

Route Directions

0.0 Park at Rancho del Oso trailhead and ride into the parking lot and past the visitor center. *Supplies are available in Davenport.*

0.4 Pass the Rancho del Oso nature center (open most weekends).

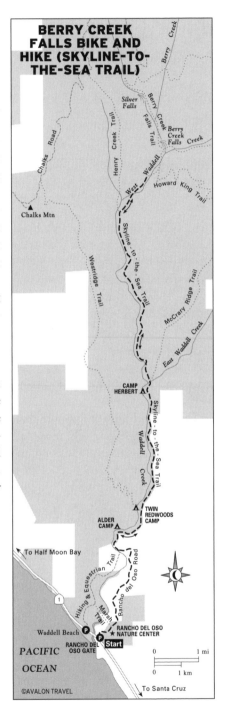

3.0 Trail washout creates tricky section with tight switchbacks. May have to walk your bike.

3.3 Cross Waddell Creek; follow the single-track trail on the right to a bridge if the stream is too high to cross.

5.8 Bike rack; TURN AROUND. *Lock up your bike and follow the hiking trail across the creek for 0.6 mile to Berry Creek Falls.*

11.6 Arrive at starting point.

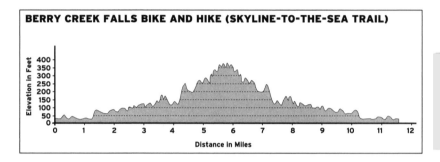

BERRY CREEK FALLS BIKE AND HIKE (SKYLINE-TO-THE-SEA TRAIL)

RESOURCES

Bay Area Bike Clubs

Looking for some friends to ride with? Check out these Bay Area bike clubs:

Bay Area
Bay Area Velo Girls
www.velogirls.com

North Bay
Bicycle Trails Council of Marin (Marin)
www.btcmarin.org

Different Spokes (San Francisco)
www.dssf.org

Golden Gate Cyclists (Marin)
www.goldengatecyclists.org

Marin Cyclists Road Club (Marin)
www.marincyclists.com

Petaluma Wheelmen (Petaluma)
www.petalumawheelmen.org

Women's Mountain Bike and Tea Society (WOMBATS) (Marin)
www.wombats.org

East Bay
Bicycle Trails Council of the East Bay (Berkeley)
www.btceb.org

Cherry City Cyclists (San Leandro)
www.cherrycitycyclists.org

Delta Pedalers Bike Club (Antioch)
www.deltaped.org

Diablo Cyclists (Walnut Creek)
www.diablocyclists.org

Grizzly Peak Cyclists (Berkeley)
www.grizzlypeakcyclists.org

Oakland Yellowjackets Bicycle Club (Oakland)
www.oaklandyellowjackets.org

Strada Sempre Duro (Walnut Creek)
www.duro.org

Valley Spokesmen (Dublin)
www.valleyspokesmen.org

Peninsula and South Bay
Almaden Cycle Touring Club (San Jose)
www.actc.org

Los Gatos Bicycle Racing Club (Los Gatos)
www.lgbrc.org

Mountain Bikers of Santa Cruz (Santa Cruz)
www.mbosc.org

Responsible Organized Mountain Pedalers (ROMP) (San Mateo and Santa Clara Counties)
www.romp.org

Western Wheelers (Palo Alto)
www.westernwheelers.org

Bay Area Bike Shops

Alameda
Alameda Bicycle
1522 Park Street
510/522-0070
www.alamedabicycle.com

Cycle City
1433 High Street
510/521-2872
www.cyclecityusa.com

Stone's Cyclery
2320 Santa Clara Avenue
510/523-3264

Alamo
Alamo Bicycles
1483 Danville Boulevard
925/837-8444

Albany
Solano Avenue Cyclery
1554 Solano Avenue
510/524-1094
www.solanoavenuecyclery.com

Antioch
Bikes 4 Life
1344 Sunset Drive
925/754-8025

Schwinn City
814 A Street
925/757-0664

Belmont
California Sports & Cyclery
1464 El Camino Real
650/593-8806

Berkeley
Berkeley Bikes & Skateboards
1227 San Pablo Avenue
510/356-4454
www.bikesandskateboards.com

Mike's Bikes
2161 University Avenue
510/845-2453
www.mikesbikes.com

Missing Link
1988 Shattuck Avenue
510/843-7471
www.missinglink.org

Recycle Bicycle
3121 Sacramento Street
510/666-1300
www.recyclebicycleshop.com

REI
1338 San Pablo Avenue
510/527-4140
www.rei.com

Solano Avenue Cyclery
1554 Solano Avenue
510/524-1094
www.solanoavenuecyclery.com

Velo Sport
1615 University Avenue
510/849-0437
www.velosportbicycles.com

Brentwood
REI
2475 Sand Creek Road
925/516-3540
www.rei.com

Burlingame
Summit Bicycles
1031 California Drive
650/343-8483
www.summitbicycles.com

Campbell
Performance Bike
1646 South Bascom Avenue
408/559-0495
www.performancebike.com

Tread
501 East Campbell Avenue
408/792-7191
www.treadbikes.com

Wheel Away Cycle Center
402 East Hamilton Avenue
408/378-4636
www.wheelaway.com

Castro Valley
AreaCycles
3052 Castro Valley Boulevard
510/589-7291
www.areacycles.com

Castro Valley Cyclery
20515 Stanton Avenue
510/538-1878
www.castrovalleycyclery.com

Eden Bicycles
3318 Village Drive
510/881-5000
www.edenbicycles.com

Endless Cycles
3300 East Castro Valley Boulevard
501/470-3551
www.endlesscyclesonline.com

Clayton
Clayton Bicycle Center
5411 Clayton Road
925/672-2522
www.encinabicyclecenters.com

Concord
REI
1975 Diamond Boulevard, B-100
Willows Shopping Center
925/825-9400
www.rei.com

Corte Madera
REI
213 Corte Madera Town Center
415/927-1938
www.rei.com

Spearhead Bicycle Excellence
79 Belvedere Street
415/342-7618
www.ride888.com

Cupertino
Cupertino Bike Shop
10493 South De Anza Boulevard
408/255-2217
www.cupertinobikeshop.com

Evolution Bike Shop
19685 Stevens Creek Boulevard
408/252-5202
www.evolutionbikeshop.com

Daly City
Mission Motion
7080 Mission Street
650/994-2456
www.missionmotion.com

Danville
California Pedaler
495 Hartz Avenue
925/820-0345
www.calped.com

Danville Bikes
115 Hartz Avenue
925/837-0966
www.danvillebikes.com

Pegasus Bicycle Works
415 Railroad Avenue
925/362-2220
www.pegasusbicycleworks.com

Dublin
Dublin Cyclery
7001 Dublin Boulevard
925/828-8676
www.dublincyclery.com

Livermore Cyclery
7214 San Ramon Road
925/829-4310
www.livermorecyclery.com

REI
7099 Amador Plaza Road
925/828-9826
www.rei.com

El Sobrante
El Sobrante Cyclery
5057 El Portal Drive
510/223-3440

The Pedaler
3826 San Pablo Dam Road
510/222-3420
www.theped.com

Fairfax
Fairfax Cyclery
2020 Sir Francis Drake Boulevard
415/721-7644
wwwfairfaxcyclery.com

Sunshine Bicycle Center
737 Center Boulevard
415/459-3334
www.sunshinebicyle.com

Fremont
The Bicycle Garage
5006 Mowry Avenue
510/795-9622
www.bicyclegarage.com

REI
43962 Fremont Boulevard
510/651-0305
www.rei.com

Half Moon Bay
The Bike Works
520 Kelly Street
650/726-6708

Hayward
Cyclepath
22510 Foothill Boulevard
510/881-5177
www.cyclepathhayward.com

Witt's Bicycle Shop
22125 Mission Boulevard
510/538-8771

Lafayette
Hank and Frank Bicycles
3377 Mount Diablo Boulevard
925/283-2453
www.hankandfrank.com

Sharp Bicycles
969 Moraga Road
925/284-9616
www.sharpbicycle.com

Larkspur
Village Peddler
1111 Magnolia Avenue
415/461-3091
www.villagepeddler.com

Livermore
Cal Bicycles
2053 First Street
925/447-6666
www.calbicycles.com

Livermore Cyclery
2752 First Street
925/455-8090
www.livermorecyclery.com

Los Altos
The Bicycle Outfitter
963 Fremont Avenue
650/948-8092 or 650/948-8126
www.bicycleoutfitter.com

Chain Reaction Bicycles
2310 Homestead Road
408/735-8735
www.chainreaction.com

Los Gatos
Crossroads Bicycles
217 North Santa Cruz Avenue
408/354-0555
www.crossroadsbicycles.com

Summit Bicycles
111 East Main Street
408/399-9142
www.summitbicycles.com

Menlo Park
Menlo Velo
433 El Camino Real
650/327-5137
www.menlovelobicycles.com

Mill Valley
Above Category
38 Millwood Street
415/389-5461
www.abovecategory.net

Studio Velo
247 Shoreline Highway
415/407-8960
www.studiovelomv.com

Tam Bikes
357 Miller Avenue
415/389-1900
www.tambikes.com

Milpitas
Sportmart/Sports Authority
111 Ranch Drive and 1200 Great Mall
Drive
408/934-0280
www.sportsauthority.com

Sun Bike Shop
1624 South Main Street
408/262-4360
www.sunbikeshop.com

Morgan Hill
Sunshine Bicycles
16825 Monterey Road
408/779-4015
www.sunshinebicycles.com

Mountain View
The Off Ramp
2320 El Camino Real
650/968-2974
www.offrampbikes.com

Performance Bike
2124 West El Camino Real
650/964-1796
www.performancebike.com

REI
2450 Charleston Road
650/969-1938
www.rei.com

Novato
Classcycle
1531-B South Novato Boulevard
415/897-3288

Road and Tri Sports
366 Bel Marin Keys Boulevard, Suite A
415/786-9181

Oakland
Bay Area Bikes
2424 Webster Street
510/763-2453
www.bayareabikes.com

Bent Spoke
6124 Telegraph Avenue
510/652-3089

Cycle Sports
3530 Grand Avenue
510/444-7900
www.cyclesportsonline.com

Hank and Frank Bicycles
6030 College Avenue
510/654-2453
www.hankandfrankbicycles.com

Pioneer Bike Shop
11 Rio Vista Avenue
510/658-8981

Wheels of Justice
2024 Mountain Boulevard
510/339-6091
www.wojcyclery.com

Palo Alto
Bike Connection
2011 El Camino Real
650/424-8034
www.bikeconnection.net

Mike's Bikes
3001 El Camino Real
650/858-7700
www.mikesbikes.com

Palo Alto Bicycles
171 University Avenue
650/328-7411
www.paloaltobicycles.com

Petaluma
Bici Sport
143 Kentucky Street
707/775-4676
www.bicisportusa.com

Petaluma Cyclery
1080 Petaluma Boulevard North
707/762-1990

Pleasant Hill
Pleasant Hill Cyclery
1100-C Contra Costa Boulevard
925/676-2667
www.pleasanthillcyclery.com

Pleasanton
Bicycles Pleasanton
537 Main Street
925/461-0905
www.bicyclespleasanton.com

Point Reyes Station
Point Reyes Outdoors
11401 State Route 1
415/663-9164
www.pointreyesoutdoors.com

Redwood City
Chain Reaction Bicycles
1451 El Camino Real
650/366-7130
www.chainreaction.com

Go Ride Bicycles
2755 El Camino Real
650/366-2453
www.goridebicycles.com

San Anselmo
Caesar's Cyclery
29 San Anselmo Avenue
415/721-0111
www.marinbikeshop.com

City Cycle
702 San Anselmo Avenue
415/454-9534
www.citycycle.com

San Carlos
REI
1119 Industrial Boulevard
650/508-2330
www.rei.com

San Francisco

American Cyclery
510 Frederick Street
415/664-4545
www.americancyclery.com

American Cyclery Too
858 Stanyan Street
415/876-4545
www.americancyclery.com

Avenue Cyclery
756 Stanyan Street
415/387-3155
www.avenuecyclery.com

Big Swingin' Cycles
2260 Van Ness Avenue
415/441-6294
www.bigswingincycles.com

The Bike Hut
Pier 40
415/543-4335
www.thebikehut.com

The Bike Kitchen
650-H Florida Street
415/647-2453
www.bikekitchen.org

Box Dog Bikes
494 14th Street
415/431-9627
www.boxdogbikes.com

Citizen Chain Bicycles
2064 Powell Street
415/796-2925
www.citizenchain.com

City Cycle
3001 Steiner Street
415/346-2242
www.citycycle.com

DD Cycles
4049 Balboa Street
415/752-7980
www.ddcycles.com

Free Wheel Bike Shop
914 Valencia Street
415/643-9213
www.thefreewheel.com

Fresh Air Bicycles
1943 Divisadero Street
415/563-4824

Heavy Metal Bike Shop
82 29th Street
415/643-3929
www.heavymetalbikeshop.com

High Trails Cyclery
1825 Polk Street
415/814-3216
www.hightrailssf.com

Lombardi's Sports
1600 Jackson Street
415/771-0600
http://lombardisports.myshopify.com

Marin Bikes Factory Store
1090 Folsom Street
415/934-8000
www.marinbikes.com

Mike's Bikes
1233 Howard Street
415/241-2453
www.mikesbikes.com

Mission Bicycle
766 Valencia Street
415/683-6166
www.missionbicycle.com

Noe Valley Cyclery
4193 24th Street
415/647-0886

Nomad Cyclery
2555 Irving Street
415/564-3568
www.nomadcyclery.com

Ocean Cyclery
1935 Ocean Avenue
415/239-5004
www.oceancyclery.com

Pacific Bicycle
345 Fourth Street
415/928-8466
www.pacbikes.com

Pedal Revolution
3085 21st Street
415/641-1264
www.pedalrevolution.com

Performance Bike
635 Brannan Street
415/856-0230
www.performancebike.com

Refried Cycles
3804 17th Street
415/621-2911
www.refriedcycles.com

REI
840 Brannan Street
415/934-1938
www.rei.com

Roaring Mouse Cycles
934 Old Mason Street, the Presidio
415/753-6272
www.roaringmousecycles.com

Sports Basement
1415 16th Street
415/437-0100
www.sportsbasement.com

Sports Basement
610 Old Mason Street, the Presidio
415/437-0100
www.sportsbasement.com

Treat Street Bicycle Works
Treat & 18th Streets
415/551-2453
www.treatstreetbicycle.com

Valencia Cyclery
1077 Valencia Street
415/550-6600 or 415/550-6601
www.valenciacyclery.com

Warm Planet Bikes
311 Townsend Street
415/974-6440
www.warmplanetbikes.com

San Jose
Bici Bike
5715 Cottle Road
408/225-0599

Bicycle Express
131 East William Street
408/998-1618
www.bicyleexpress.net

Calabazas Cyclery
6140 Bollinger Road
408/366-2453
www.calabazas.com

Fast Bicycle
2274 Alum Rock Avenue
408/251-9110
www.fastbicycleshop.com

Happy Trails Cyclery
4640 Meridian Avenue
408/265-8865
www.happytrailscyclery.com

Hyland Family Bicycles
1515 Meridian Avenue
408/269-2300
www.hylandbikes.com

La Dolce Velo
1280 The Alameda
408/244-8356
www.ladolcevelo.com

REI
400 El Paseo de Saratoga Shopping
Center
408/871-8765
www.rei.com

Slough's Bike Shoppe
260 Race Street
408/293-1616

Trail Head Cyclery
14390 Union Avenue
408/369-9666
www.trailheadcyclery.com

Willow Glen Bicycles
1016 Lincoln Avenue
408/293-2606
www.willowglenbicycles.com

San Leandro
Robinson Wheel Works
1235 MacArthur Boulevard
510/352-4663
www.robinsonww.com

Sports Authority
1933 Davis Street
510/632-6100
www.sportsauthority.com

San Mateo
Cyclepath
1212 South El Camino Real
650/341-0922
www.cyclepathsm.com

Talbots Cyclery
445 South B Street
650/931-8120
www.talbotscyclery.com

San Rafael
Mike's Bicycle Center
1601 Fourth Street
415/454-3747
www.mikesbikes.com

Performance Bike
369 Third Street
415/454-9063
www.performancebike.com

The Re-Cyclery
610 Fourth Street
415/458-2986

Summit Bicycles
1820 Fourth Street
415/456-4700
www.summitbicycles.com

Santa Clara
Calmar Bicycles
2236 El Camino Real
408/249-6907
www.calmarcycles.com

The Off Ramp
2369 El Camino Real
408/249-2848
www.offrampbikes.com

Sausalito
A Bicycle Odyssey
1417 Bridgeway
415/332-3050
www.bicycleodyssey.com

Mike's Bikes
1 Gate Six Road
415/332-3200
www.mikesbikes.com

Sunnyvale
Sportmart/Sports Authority
125 East El Camino Real
408/732-6400
www.sportsauthority.com

Sports Basement
1177 Kern Avenue
408/732-0300
www.sportsbasement.com

Walt's Cycles
116 Carroll Street
408/739-4287
www.waltscycles.com

Vallejo
Authorized Bicycles
1220 Georgia Street
707/648-1413

Walnut Creek
Encina Bicycle Center
2901 Ygnacio Valley Road
925/944-9200
www.encinabicyclecenters.com

Performance Bike
1401 North Broadway
925/937-7723
www.performancebike.com

Rivendell Bicycle Works
2040 North Main Street
925/933-7304
www.rivbike.com

Index

www.moon.com

MOON.COM is ready to help plan your next trip! Filled with fresh trip ideas and strategies, author interviews, informative travel blogs, a detailed map library, and descriptions of all the Moon guidebooks, Moon.com is all you need to get out and explore the world—or even places in your own backyard. While at Moon.com, sign up for our monthly e-newsletter for updates on new releases, travel tips, and expert advice from our on-the-go Moon authors. As always, when you travel with Moon, expect an experience that is uncommon and truly unique.

KEEP UP WITH MOON ON FACEBOOK AND TWITTER
JOIN THE MOON PHOTO GROUP ON FLICKR